EXCERPTS FROM THE EARLIEST MASON COUNTY, KENTUCKY NEWSPAPERS

The Mirror

1799

May 31; June 14 and 28; July 5, 10, 17 and 24; August 7-28; September 4-25; October 9-30; and November 6, 17 and 20

and

The Maysville Eagle

1818

July 15 and September 17

and

1825

March 16 and 23

Rachelle Winters-Ibrahim

HERITAGE BOOKS
2006

HERITAGE BOOKS
AN IMPRINT OF HERITAGE BOOKS, INC.

Books, CDs, and more—Worldwide

For our listing of thousands of titles see our website at
www.HeritageBooks.com

Published 2006 by
HERITAGE BOOKS, INC.
Publishing Division
65 East Main Street
Westminster, Maryland 21157-5026

Copyright © 2006 Rachelle Winters-Ibrahim

Other books by the author:
Newspaper Excerpts from the Maysville Eagle,
Mason County, Kentucky, 1827-1847

All rights reserved. No part of this book may be reproduced or transmitted in any form or by any means, electronic or mechanical, including photocopying, recording or by any information storage and retrieval system without written permission from the author, except for the inclusion of brief quotations in a review.

International Standard Book Number: 978-0-7884-3190-0

For my mother, Midge Winters, who started me on this journey, my sister, Sharon Gibson, and my brother, Michael McClanahan and all the others who have gone before me.

To the family I have left; my father, Robert Winters, my sister, Linda Easter and my brother Bob Winters.

To my Husband, Mo, and my children, Zach, Noah, Jaffer, Joseph and Adam, for believing in my work and giving me the time and resources to do it.

To Margaret Baldaulf, for helping me in my never ending quest to find Christopher.

And lastly, to Christopher Forts, 1734-1843 who died in Lewis County, Kentucky,
> my brick wall…. for keeping me going.

Special thanks to Roger Hamperian Reformatting Librarian, Margaret I. King Library University of Kentucky
The University of Kentucky Reprographics
Their URL for searching early newspapers on microfilm is
http://lib.uky.edu/repro/

The Mirror was established September 16, 1797 by Hunter and William H. Beaumont. They also established *The Palladium* at Frankfort on August 9, 1798 and published the two papers simultaneously until December 19, 1799, when *The Mirror* was discontinued.

The microfilm was filmed by the M.I. King library at the University of Kentucky at Lexington, Kentucky February 11, 1974.

This film was produced from the best and most complete file of original issues available at the time of filming. The following dates are included in 1799
May 31 (v.2, #90), June 14 and 28, July 5, 10, 17 and 24 ,August 7, 14, 21 and 28 September 4, 11, 18 and 25, October 9, 16, 23 and 30, November 6, 20 and 27.

The *Mirror's* slogan was "Firm, Free, and Temperate."
The subscription price was three dollars fee per annum.

The *Eagle* was published by Crooks Shanks, At two dollars and Fifty cents, "if paid within three months from the receipt of the first number or three dollars at the expiration of the years or for 52 numbers". The following dates are included for 1818, July 15, Sept 17, and for 1825, Mar. 16 and 23.

In these newspapers I was surprised to find so much information on foreign wars. "Buonaparte" was often written about and letters that he wrote were published in the *Mirror*.
Also political excerpts from letters sent to Kentuckians from Europe were published.

More then one article stated "A gentleman here received a letter recently from…" places ranged from all over Europe. The excerpts from letters I did not put in this work for the main reason that the excerpted text was usually political or about the war in Europe. No names were ever mentioned much to my dismay.

I have also included some accounts from other towns and communities that were written in the newspaper that did not include names but interesting facts about the peoples lives in 1799.

For political persons in the first convention I did not include their speeches which were published in whole. Some took up whole pages in the newspapers.

I used the original spelling unless I was positive that it was a typo. In the 1799 newspapers especially old English was used. I did not however change the names that were misspelled. The best example was Daviel, which I think is probably Daniel, but his name could have possibly have been Daviel so I left it as is.

Some of the newspapers were very hard to read and some parts were burned out, in that case I ended the article with …..

The Mirror, Washington Kentucky   The Eagle, Maysville, Kentucky

Friday, May 31st, 1799.

Extract of a letter from Cincinnati, to a gentleman in Philadelphia, dated April 10, 1799. "A Mr. M'Rea arrived here last evening from Natchez; he was employed in an express by Abijah Hunt, to bring a large quantity of bills of exchange from that place to this; and advanced from the Natchez as far as the river Tennessee, was there encamped on the 9th of March last, with four other travelers; when about midnight, five armed Indians seized and tied Mr. M'Rea and two of his fellow travelers; in the man time the other two escaped and fled from the camp, - The Indians, after having led their captives out and fastened them to trees, packed up every single article belonging to them, saddled and loaded their valuable horses and mounted and rode off. Mr. M'Rea and the other two built a raft and descended the river to flee; and in four days arrived at Massac, from whence he reached this place on foot last evening. Being robbed of all letters as well as bills. Mr. M'Rea can give no description of the bills, but says, that the amount is about 20,000 dollars: These bills have been collected at the Natchez by Mr. Abijah Hunt, are probably composed of Guron's bills on the Secretary of War for the pay of the army. - Of Mr. Harrigan's bills on James O'Hara or William Bell of Philadelphia - of Mr. Ellicot's bills on the treasury of the United States- and of bills drawn by or upon John Wilkins, the quarter master general's and as they have been in circulation at Natchez, there is a probability that they are endorsed in black so as to be current and demandable by their bearer. This is all the information that at present we are possessed of;; but it is highly probable, that in a few days,, Mr. Jesse Hunt, of this place to whom the lost bills were addressed, will receive duplicates, and such further information from Natchez, as will enable him to furnish more complete information towards detection and stoppage of payments."

Lexington, May 21. By a gentleman just arrived from Fort Massac, we have been favored with the following important information- That he saw a letter from a respectable gentleman in Kaskaskia, to the commandant of that post, which mentioned the certainty of four nations of Indians (the names of whom he does not recollect, but they reside above the Illinois river and northwardly of that river) being hostile to the people of Kaskaskia, and particularly to the tribe of Kaskaskia Indians, several of whom they have taken and killed within this spring - that the people of the Illinois settlement appear much alarmed, as also the Kaskaskia Indians.

The Mirror, Washington Kentucky   The Eagle, Maysville, Kentucky

The Mirror. Washington, May 31. Several reports have been in circulation respecting hostilities on the part of the Indians, which has occasioned some degree of alarm among the frontier settlers. We are happy to have it in our power to announce that there is no real foundation for such reports. A letter we have just received from a gentleman in Chillicotha, whose information we think must be good, enables us to speak positively on the subject.

Mr. Davis has been returned to Congress, from the South side of Kentucky river, by a very decided majority.

Virginia Returns. In addition to the list of new members, which we gave last week, we are now enabled to add the following viz. Clay, New, Cable, Randolph, Gray and Evans. The district before represented by J. Trigg is the only one from which the returns are not yet received - his re-election is very probably.

The trial of the unfortunate Fries of Northampton, is concluded - he has been found guilty - Sentence had not been passed on him, at the date of the latest Philadelphia papers we received, by the last mail. The trial of the others, against whom bills have been found by the grand Jury, had not come on.

Caution. As there is much danger in passing the Rapids of Ohio, and as I am appointed as Pilot, by Act of Assembly, for the purpose of navigating Boats and other Craft, down and up the same, consider it my duty to inform those Gentlemen who are strangers to the Channel, to beware of ignorant persons who may attempt to pilot their boats through the Rapids. I have given bond for 2 proper discharge of my duty, and consider myself responsible for such losses as may happen by my neglect, or for want of skill in the business. James Patten.

Taken up by the subscriber living on the waters of Lawrence Creek, a dark bay hose about 14 hands high, shod all round, has a star and a small ?, also a feather on the oft side of his withers, and either a brand or sear on his near shoulder, about 12 years old. Appraised to f 10. William Crosby.

For Sale. By the subscriber a tract of very valuable land lying to the North West side of Ohio, within five or six miles of the Falls of Paint Creek. One of the tracts contains 1100 acres and the other 840. They will be divided into smaller tracts to accommodate purchasers. More particular

The Mirror, Washington Kentucky   The Eagle, Maysville, Kentucky

information of the quality and situation of the land may be obtained, and the terms known, by application to Col. Massie. John Thompson

For Sale, all my lands lying on Fox's creek; being part of Lots 7, 10 and 12, in Mosby's survey of 30,000 Acres. It is unnecessary to describe these lands, as the purchaser will wish first to see them - It will suffice to remark, that the quality of the soil is good, the range for flock uncommonly fine, the situation healthy, and the title indisputable. For the purpose of suiting purchasers in tracts of any size, I have empowered Mr. John Winn, living near Washington, to show and sell said land. Such persons as may have purchased any part of the above lots of B? Ramsay are here by directed The rest is torn by Thomas

Lands for sale in the State of Kentucky. 52, 217 Acres on Paint Creek, waters of Big Sandy, Fleming county. 40,000- on Saxton Creek about ten miles above three forks of Kentucky river. 520,000 on Nolin and Rock Creek, in Harden county. 15,331 on Rough Creek, Harden county. 5,000 On the same creek. 500 Near the Ohio in said county. 20,000 on Rock Creek, a branch of Nolin. 5,000 In Fayette County. 7,000 in 7 different surveys lying on and near the Licking River, between the Upper and Lower blue licks. The whole or any part of the above lands I will sell for cash, or on a long credit Persons settling on the lands will have a preference.. Also, 10,000 acres on Little Sandy River, Mason County. 3,900 on the waters of Licking near Cincinnati in Campbell County. 7,500 On Barklick Creek in said County. 5,600 On Eagle Creek, Franklin County. 2,250 on Ashes Creek Washington County. 8,000 On the Ohio in Harden Co. 3,000 on and near the Wabash River at Post Vennens in the North Western Territory. For these lands, I will take in payment: Negroes, Horses, Cattle, Merchandise or Country Produce. Application personally or by letters post paid to David Barber. Who keeps an office for transacting land business in its different branches.

Take Notice. The trustees of the Methodist meeting house, in Flemingsburgh, take this method to lay before their friends and brethren, the size state and situation of the business of that house. The size twenty eight feet by thirty-six; standing on one acre lot in the Town of Flemingsburgh, given gratis (together with ten pounds,, by Maj. George Stockton, Boarding, stalling and other services done by said Stockton gratis; the house built with brick, a good gallery on two sides and one end now up, the walls are raised two feet above the same. The balance of the brick is made; ten windows.. the rest in unreadable and torn.

The Mirror, Washington Kentucky   The Eagle, Maysville, Kentucky

February Term 1799. State of Kentucky, Washington District, Thomas Waring & al, against Robert Meck and Mary his wife, James Wood and Katy his wife, John Wood and Mary his wife, Alex. Smith and Anne his wife, heirs and representatives of Nath. Allen deceased, John Machir assignee of said Allen, Thomas Sloo and David Brodrick, George Lewis and William JenningIt appearing to the satisfaction of the court that the defendants Robert Meck and Mary his wife, James Wood ad Katy his wife, John Wood and Mary his wife, Alex. Smith and Anne his wife, heirs and representatives of Nathaniel Allen deceased, are not inhabitants of this commonwealth; on the motion of he complainants, by their attorney, it is ordered that the said defendants appear here on the third day of the next Term and answer the complainant's Bill, and that a copy of this ordered be inserted in the Mirror, two months successively, another posted at the door of the court house in Mason county, and that this order be published some Sunday, at the door of the Baptist Meeting House in Washington. Teste, Francis Taylor, C.W.D.C.

High-Flyer, A beautiful Dapple Gray, full sixteen hands high, now in full perfection, will stand at the stable of Mr. Robert Walker, in Montgomery County, three miles from Mountsterling, on the road leading from thence to Paris, and will be let to Mares the ensuing season, which will commence the first of April, and end the fifteen of July, at sever dollars the season, four the single leap, and thirteen to ensure a Mare with foal. The following articles will be received in payment, if delivered at the stand before Christmas, at the market price of such articles, to wit, Hemp, Beef Cattle or young Cattle, Pork, Country Linen or Sugar; but five dollars will be discharge the season of each Mare, if paid in Cash; before the expiration thereof, and three dollars, the single leap, paid also in the season. We think it unnecessary to say much respecting the figure, strength and activity of High Flyer, as he will be seen at the Court Houses of Montgomery and Clark Counties, and perhaps other places, where gentlemen who please to favor us with their custom, may be an eye witness of his beauty and elegance, his blood being given up, by all who know him, to equal that of any horse ever bred on the continent, and for information to those who do not, we infer the following Pedigree, which can be proven by gentlemen of respectability both in this state and Virginia. James & John Mason.

High Flyer was get by the imported hose High Flyer, his dam by Col. Bailor's old Fearnought, his grandam by Monkey. His great grandam by Childers, his great great grandam by the imported horse Dancing master out

The Mirror, Washington Kentucky   The Eagle, Maysville, Kentucky

of Col. Allen's imported running mare, Creeping Cate.   Resly Thornton
Teste. Hubard Taylor.   Anthony Thornton
I do certify that High flyer, a dapple gray hose, late the property of Captain Presly Thornton of Essex County, Virginia, and sold by him to James and John Mason of this state, is a sure and good foal getter, his colts are as likely as any ever dropped in the neighborhood of Frankfort, he having been in my possession for two seasons past. Given under my hand this 17th day of March, 1799. William Owens. Teste, Bennett Pemberton, Giles Samuel..

Strayed, from the town of Washington, about ten days or a fortnight since two cows. One White, with a pair of wide ? and giving milk, the other a ? bodied brindle cow, narrow horns, as is supposed from her calving. Information where these cowd are ? paid by W. H. Beaumont.

Mason County, April Term 1799. Meeker & Cochran, of the house & firm of Meeker Cochran & Co. against James and William Armstrong. Defendants. It appearing to the satisfaction of this court that the defendant William Armstrong, is not an inhabitant of this commonwealth; and he not appearing to answer the complainants bill agreeable to law and the rules of this court upon the motion of the complainants, by their attorney, it is ordered that he appear here at the next August Court on the first day thereof in person or by some attorney of said court and answer the said bill, or the same shall be taken as confessed, and it is further ordered that a copy of this order be inserted in the Mirror, two months successively, another posted at the door of the Court House in mason County, and that this order be published some Sunday, at the door of the Baptist Meeting House in Washington. Test, Thomas Marshall. J. C. M. C.

Notice. I shall petition the worshipful court of Bourbon at their next June term for leave to lay off a town on my land, on the main road, leading from the Upper Blue Lick to Paris - Agreeable to an act, entitled an act, for the better establishing of towns. Benjamin Hall.

Friday, June 14, 1799

Interesting East-India Intelligence, extracted from letters addressed to the Editor of the Aurora, who formerly resided in that Country Hindustan.

We have before us a letter from Gen. Desfourneaux, to an old acquaintance, which he acquired in this city during his residence here. As the language of

The Mirror, Washington Kentucky   The Eagle, Maysville, Kentucky

private friendship is generally better criterion of the humane disposition than the language of diplomacy, for when they concur in one object it is impossible to refute our credit to the sincerity of the letter corroborated by the former. Document torn, the general talks about Guadaloupe.

Extract of a letter from the Rev. Mr. Nelson, father of the Baron of the Nile, to the Rev. Mr. Brian Allot, (Who is living in the neighborhood of Burnham) in answer to a congratulatory Episode on the late Victory, dated October, 1798.) "My great and good son went into the world without fortune, but with a heart replete with every moral and religious virtue, these have been his compass to steer by: an it has pleased God to be his shield in the days of battle, and to give success to his wishes, to be of service to his country.". "His country seems sensible of his services - but should he ever meet with ingratitude, his scars will cry out and plead his cause - for at the siege of Bastia he lost an eye, at Tenerisse an arm. On the memorable 14th of Feb. he received a severe blow on his body, which he still feels, and now a wound on his head. After all this you will believe his bloom of countenance must be faded, but the spirit breath yet as vigorous as ever. " On the 29th of last month (Sept.) he completed his fortieth year; cheerful, generous and good, fearing no evil be cause he has done none, an honor to my gray hairs which with every mark of old age, creep fast upon me."

Domestic Intelligence. New York, May 18: A gentleman who arrived here on Thursday last from New Orleans, informs us, that on the 22nd of April, a company of seventy American troops, under the command of Captain Shamber, passed through that place for Mobillo, to take possession of the lines. Mr. Ellicot, the United states surveyor general, left New Orleans a few days before.

Baltimore, May 17. Melancholy. On Wednesday evening a poor disconsolate woman, seemingly delirious, with a beautiful female infant, about five months old, was observed on *Valck's wharf*, by persons passing that way; they had not time to approach her until she plunged with her infant into the water; by their united efforts, they however saved both from drowning, and brought her to the house of Godfried Hartung, in *Cambden street*, were every thing possible was done to restore her to resignation, but all in vain - giving her infant in solemn charge to Mrs. Hartung, after complaining of sickness and retiring to rest, she found means of going to the attick story and about nice o'clock yesterday morning threw herself from a window about sixty feet high; and broke her thigh, her arm, and breast bone. She lingered about an hour and an half, and then expired. She is said to be the wife of a man named Boyce, who sailed from this port about eight months

The Mirror, Washington Kentucky   The Eagle, Maysville, Kentucky

since, and the reason assigned for the above melancholy accident, is the report of his loss at sea. Mrs. Hartung, at present, has the child under her protection. Humanity here calls aloud for the assistance of all well disposed persons; and hopes are entered, that amongst established societies in this city something may be done towards the support of the hapless innocent, thrown on the world, deprived of parents, and trusting only to the mercy of those, whom the untimely fate of a mother has caused to be a protector

[1]*Philadelpiha*, May 18th in the circuit Court. This morning. Judge Iredell, after addressing the following name persons on the heinousness of the offenses, of which they had been severally convicted pronounced the following judgments: George Sheffers, convicted of conspiracy and obstruction of process , to pay a fine for the first offense, viz. The conspiracy, of 400 dollars, and be imprisoned for 8 months; for the second offense, viz. Obstruction of process, to pay a fine of 200 dollars, and be imprisoned 4 months. To give security in himself of 1000 dollars, and two sureties of 500 dollars each, for his good behavior for two years, from the expiration of the period of his imprisonment. Daniel Schwartz, Sen. Convicted of conspiracy, to pay a fine of 400 dollars and to be imprisoned for 8 months; also to give security as above for his good behavior for one year. Christian Ruth and Henry Stahler, convicted of Refcue, to pay a fine of 200 dollars each, and to be imprisoned for 8 months; also to give security as above. Henry Schiffer, convicted of Refcue, to pay a fine of 50 dollars and to be imprisoned for 8 months; to give sureties of 250 dollars each for his good behavior for two years. All and each of the above defendants to stand committed, until their sentences be complied with. The Court, taking into consideration the circumstances of the parties, proportioned the penalties to the capacity of each. Yesterday morning, Mr. Lewis, concluded the pleadings in support of his motion for granting to the unfortunate John Fries; a new trial, to which the court consented - which is expected will take place in October next.

Washington, June 4. Died, in this place, on Wednesday last, after a long and grievous sickness, Mrs. Tebbs, wife of Samuel Tebbs

The Ocean - Kemp. Captian Kemp, who was reported to have been murdered by the crews of some French privateers, (and concerning whose

---

[1] As spelled in the paper

The Mirror, Washington Kentucky   The Eagle, Maysville, Kentucky

fate the public attention had been considerably awalged) arrived yesterday in the ship Ocean, from Very Cruz, in 25 days, and anchored in the North river. Capt. Kempt,[2] from La Vera Cruz, informs, that a Spanish fleet of two sail of the line, and several frigates, sailed from Vera Cruz, for the *Havannah,* where they had arrived, having on board 30,000,000 dollars

Quarry of Plaister of Paris. A Quarry of stone equal in virtue to Plaister of Paris, has been discovered on the farm of Mr. John Dill, in *York county,* about ten miles from *Carlisle,* and from actual trial made by several respectable farmers allod to be equal to that imported

From *Wilmington,* (*N. Carolina* paper). Useful and new inventions are a subject that has occupied the attention of the government of the United States, & one of an extraordinary nature has made its appearance here. Mr. Joseph Belton has made a GUN (at least he is the inventor) that will receive four charges at once, and fire them all separately & upon the same plan he can make one & intends to do so, that will fire 2 rounds in two minutes. He has several times fired the one he has finished to the astonishment of all who saw it. It fires regularly one load after another with the single motion of the forefinger, just giving time for the person to take sight at the object. It is as much superior to the common gun, as that is to the bow and arrow. Mr. Belton intends shortly to go to the *Philadelphia* with his model, or rather his gun actually completed, where there is no doubt he will meet with encouragement This may appear a little extraordinary to the public, but the thing is done ad speaks for itself. It is upon the most simple construction, and will cost not one dollar more than the common gun. It is truly republican. Mr. Belton is a native of *Connecticut,* near *New London,* but has resided at *Lumberton* upwards of six years. I hope he will receive the reward of his merit. He is an unexceptionable good character.

The Subscriber is now opening for sale, a handsome assortment of Dry Goods, Groceries; Hard Ware & Pewter, at his Mills, lately know by *Wood's Mount Pleasant Mills,* two miles from Limestone; which he is determined to sell low for cash; and will take for Dry Goods and Hard Ware, Corn, Bacon, Country Linen, Wheat & Tobacco'; John Edwards. Sen. June 12th 1799

---

2 name spelled differently the second time.

The Mirror, Washington Kentucky   The Eagle, Maysville, Kentucky

To all whom it may concern. Take notice, that I shall attend on Tuesday the 9th of July, with Commissioners appointed by the Worshipful Court of Fleming County, at the improvement of John Jones on Fleming Creek, to take depositions for establishing the said improvement and specials cases of John Jones' preemption, and do such farther and other things as may be necessary under the law. William Kennan, party concerned in said claim.

Notice, Is Hereby given, that on Monday the first day of July, that I shall proceed to take the depositions of sundry witnesses to establish the beginning of an entry in the name of John Tabb, in *Bourbon county*, and on the waters of *Hinkston*, that calls for two Ash Saplins growing from one root; with the letter K marked on each of them, and standing at the fork of a branch and on the East side thereof, and four or five miles nearly north East of *Harrod's lick* - and do such other acts as the Commissioners may think proper, and agreeable to law. Philemon Thomas. June 10th 1799

Lands For Sale. In the State of Kentucky. 52,217 Acres on Paint Creek, waters of Big Sandy Fleming county. 50,000 On Saxton Creek about ten miles above the three forks of Kentucky river. 51,000 On Nolin and Rock Creek, in Harden County. 15,331 On Rough Creek Harden County. 5,000 On the fame creek. 500 Near the Ohio in said County. 20000 On Rock Creek, a branch of Nolin. 5,000 In Fayette County. 7,000 In 7 different surveys lying on and near the Licking River, between the upper and Lower blue licks. The whole or any part of the above ands I will sell for cash, or on a long Credit. Persons settling on the Lands will have a preference. Also 10,000 acres on Little Sandy River Mason County, 3,900 On the waters of Licking near Cincinnati in Campbell county. 7,500 on Banklick Creek in said County 5,600 On Eagle Creek, Franklin county. 2,250 On. Ashes Creek, Washington County. 8,000 On the Ohio in Harden Co. 3,000 On and near the Wabash Ro. Verat Post Vennens in the North Western Territory. For these ads I will take in payment: Negros, Horses, Cattle, Merchandise or Country Produce. Application personally or by letters post paid to David Barber Louisville, May 18th 1799. David Barber Who keeps an office for transacting Land Business in its different branches

For Sale by the subscriber, two tracts of very valuable Land lying on the North West side of *Ohio,* within five or six Miles of the *Falls of Paint Creek.* One of the tracts contains 1100 Acres and the other 840. They will be divided into smaller tracts to accommodate purchasers. More particular information of the quality and situation of the Land may be obtained, and

The Mirror, Washington Kentucky   The Eagle, Maysville, Kentucky

the terms known, by application to Col. Massie.   John Thompson, Jefferson, March 20th 1799.

A TAVERN. I wish to inform my friends and the public in general, that I have opened a public House in the town of *Chilicotha* N. W. Territory, the Sign of the Red Lyon, Water Street. And have it in my power to accommodate Travellers with any necessary they may stand in need of on the most reasonable terms. I always keep on hand a supply of Corn, Oats and Hay - Good Stabling and pasturage; and supply travelers that are going through the wilderness with suitable provisions, & c. to carry with them - and shall make it my study to merit the approbation of those who will please to favor me with their custom. William Keys. Chilicotha June 3rd 1799

I Will Sell A Prime Tract of Lad of three hundred acres on *Cabin Creek*, including the forks, on which are about one hundred and fifty acres of excellent bottom. The whole will be disposed of together or in parts, to suit those who may wish to purchase, and a general warrantee deed, given. For particulars respecting the terms, apply to me in Mason county. Charles Pelham. June 3, 1799

To all whom it may concern. Take notice, that the purchasers under the preemption of Philip Pendleton Asse. Of Wm. McCleary, will attend at his improvement on the North Fork of Licking above the mouth of *Pharo's Creek*. With commissioners appointed by the County Court of *Mason,* on the first day of July next, then and there to take depositions for perpetuating testimony respecting the said improvement and boundaries, and to do such other things as the law directs. Archibald Wiggins. June 3rd 1799

Mason County, ss. Robert B. Morton, against Bertrand & Jesse Ewell, Chars. Pelham, Wm. Wood and Raweigh Chinn It appearing to the satisfaction of this court that Bertrand and Jesse Ewell are not inhabitants of this Commonwealth, and they having failed to enter their appearance agreeable to Law and the rules of this Court; upon the motion of the Complainants by his Attorney, It is ordered that unless they do appear here, on the first day of the next August Court, in person, or by some Attorney of said court, and answer the said Complainant's bill, the same will be taken as confessed, and it is further ordered that a copy of this order be advertised in the Mirror, two month successively, another posted at the Baptist meeting House, in Washington some Sunday immediately, after

The Mirror, Washington Kentucky   The Eagle, Maysville, Kentucky

divine service, and a third at the door of the Court House in said Town. (A copy) Teste, Thomas Marshall, j. C. M.C.

We are desired to mention, that there is a letter deposited att he office of the Mirror, for a certain James Austain - said to reside either in Fayette or Bourbon Counties Kentucky It is understood to be of considerable consequence tot he person to whom directed. Mirror Ed.

GREAT BARGAINS. To be had at the next District Court. Will be sold at auction, at the Court House in *Washington*; three valuable Horses, proved to be good, having been employed in carrying the Mail thr' the Wilderness. They being the property of the General Post Office, No notes with security will be asked. Ready cash will be the purchaser. Ed. Harris, P.M. Washington, June 4, 1799

Taken up by the subscriber living on the waters of *Lawrence's Creek*, a dark bay horse about 14 hands high, saod all round, has a star and small snip also a feather on the off side of his withers, has either a brand or scar on his near shoulder, about 12 years old.   Appraised to 10 £   May 27th 1799. William Crosby

To all whom it may concern. Take notice, that the purchasers under the preemption of Terel & Hawkins assee of John Fitzpatrick, will attend at his improvement with commissioners appointed by the county court of *Mason*, on the twenty 6th of June next, then and there to take depositions for perpetuating testimony respecting the said improvement and to do such other things as the law directs. Joseph Desha April 24th

For Sale, All my lands lying on Fox's creek, being part of Lots 7, 10 and 12, in Mosby's survey of 30,000 Acres. It is unnecessary to describe these lands, as the purchaser will wish first to see them.It will suffice to remark, that the quality of the soil is good , the situation healthy, and the title indisputable. For the purpose of suiting purchasers in tracts of any size, I have empowered Mr. John Winn, living near *Washington* , to show and fell the said Land. Such persons as may have purchased any part of the above lots of Burke and Ramsay, are hereby directed to pay off the sums respectively due on their bonds, which are now lodged with Mr. Winn for collection. Should they not immediately avail themselves of this notice, they may expect the land will be sold to others and they turned out of possession. Thomas Hart, Sen. September 18th 1798

The Mirror, Washington Kentucky   The Eagle, Maysville, Kentucky

Mason County, April Term 1799. MEEKER & COCHRAN, of the house & firm of Meeker Cochran & Co. Against James and William Armstrong. It Appearing to the satisfaction of this court that the defendant William Armstrong, is not an inhabitant of this commonwealth; and he not appearing to answer the complainants bill agreeable to law and the rules of this Court upon the motion of the complainants, by their attorney, it is ordered that he appear here at the next August Court on the first day there or in person or by some attorney of said Court and answer the said bill, or the same shall be taken as confessed, and it is further ordered that a copy of this order be inserted in the *Mirror*, two months successively, another posted at the door of the Court house in *Mason County*, and that this order be published some Sunday, at the door of the Baptist Meeting House in Washington, Test, Thomas Marshall j. C. M. C.

Friday June 28th 1799.

Letter from George Logan about his 500 mile travel through France.

Washington, (Pen.) May 20. Commonwealth against Andrew M'Clure. Last Monday commenced the trial of Mr. Andrew M'Clure, on an indictment for an assault upon the person of Alexander Addison, Esq. Before the court of Nisi Prius, holden at this place. The testimony on the part of the defendant was as follows: On the day of the last annual election, a number of peaceable citizens were investigating the characters and conduct of the respective candidates for the congress of the United States, advancing reasons for their opinions, &c-When Mr. Addison, rather in an insolent manner, obtruded himself into their company, and insisted upon a young gentleman, a friend of his, to leave the crowd, when Mr. M'Clure observed, that he hoped every citizen would on that day exercise his wn opinion, and vote for whom he pleased: where upon Mr. Addison immediately rejoined-"Who hinders you to vote for whom you please you damn'd (or insignificant) puppy." Some opprobrious epithets passed from one to the other when Mr. Addison, who too frequently looses sight of reason and discretion, made a push or stroke at Mr. M'Clure, and as appeared by the testimony immediately assaulted him previous to any blow given by Mr. M'Clure. At this instant the young gentleman gave his Honor a blow which leveled him to the ground, he then inagnanimousy profered him his hand, to raise him from his humble situation, and as soon as he was brought upon his centre, another bow caused him again to lick the dust. Mr. Addison was then carried off. These are the facts, in substance as stated by the witnesses. Every dispassionate man must perceive, that Mr.

The Mirror, Washington Kentucky   The Eagle, Maysville, Kentucky

M'Clure acted with the greatest moderation and discretion, even permitting Mr. A. to term him a ---- puppy, and also to receive an Unprovoked assault, before he committed the battery, in which he was perfectly justifiable, by the laws of self defense. Probably it may not be improper to state that Mr. Addison swore pointedly that he was calm, cool, dispassionate, and at the same time acknowledged that he called him a puppy, Also, that the first assault was given by Mr. M'Clure, when there were ten reputable witnesses who gave their testimony differently, and swore positively, the Mr. Addison gave the most provoking language; as well as the first assault. These things would have been some time ago difficult to recondle. After the witnesses had been examined and the counsel for the Defendant, (Mr. Brackenridge) had in a modest, but masterly manner, with his usual perspicuity and precision exhibited every circumstance in its true light, the honorable Judge Yeartes, in a decent forcible, temperate and gentlemanly address to the jury, impressed it upon their minds, that although every person in the court would be willing to give full credit to Mr. Addison as a man - yet that passion to frequently obtains an ascendancy over reason, that in all probability, at the time, Mr. Addison might not with accuracy recollect his giving the first push, but there was a cloud of witnesses, who, though they had differed in smaller Circumstances, yet all agreed that Mr. Addison had given, what they termed, the first assault. He likewise touched forcibly upon the right of election, observing that free discussion and investigation was the true method to obtain a good representation, and that any interference or attempt to abridge that right was a violation of the Constitution. The Jury retired and in a few minutes bro't in their verdict NOT GUILTY. We may further remark that Mr. Addison himself issued the warrant for the apprehension of Mr. M'Clure; that he took the bail for his appearance, thereby becoming Judge in his own cause. Decency it might have been supposed would have pointed out a different line of conduct. Whether under every circumstance, this can be termed a malicious prosecution, we will not pretend to say; but this may be observed that so many circumstances combine, as induce a belief that a suit can, and possibly may be instituted against Mr. Addison for damages.

The following singular incident happened in the state of Vermont the last summer. Mr. Loudon Case, of Addison, was riding with his sister on horseback, from Waterbury to Stowe: Their road lay through a long piece of wood - when they were about half way through, and at four miles distance from any house, they were overtaken by a gentleman well dressed, and mounted on a spirited horse who joined the travelers, and politely bowing, entered into a very amusing conversation: The party soon came to

The Mirror, Washington Kentucky   The Eagle, Maysville, Kentucky

a very fine spring, where they all stopped to water their horses. The stranger immediately sprung from his horse and observed "that he had a loaded pistol in his saddle bags, and that he did not know that he could have a better time to discharge it." Mr. Case immediately took the alarm, and while the highwayman was searching for his pistol, struck his sister's horse and putting spurs to his own, set off full gallop. The stranger repeatedly called to them to stop! But Mr. Case looking round, observed that he held the loaded pistol in his hand, struck his spurs deeper and fled for life. The stranger mounted his horse and pursued - He soon overtook the young lady, and begged her as he passed for God's sake not be frightened, rode at full speed after the brother, beseeching him to stop and not be frightened, declaring that he intended him no harm. Mr. Case, after dropping his had and portmanteau happily arrived safe in Stowe. He immediately alarmed the inhabitants, who with great bravery, activity and spirit, apprehended the highwayman: but upon searching him, no pistol was found upon him; his saddlebags contained only a case of surgical instruments; some necessary linen, and a small bottle of excellent Jamaica spirits;. This last article it seems, give rise to Mr. Case's perturbation. The highwayman proved to be a physician of eminence and character from the neighboring town of Cambridge, and it seems merely intended to invite Mr. Case to partake of his Jamaica spirits; calling the half pint bottle by the common cant name of pistol. Mr. Case's hat and portmanteau were found safe in the road the next day; and we understand the young lady suffered no lasting injury from her alarm; not being so much frightened as her brother. In newspaper phrase, "This should be a solemn warning to people traveling not to make use of metaphors."

We find it necessary to intimate to all persons indebted to the Office of the Mirror for subscription, advertising or otherwise, that payment is expected to be made prior to the twenty-first day of July next. All who are at that time, more than six months in arrears, except such of our subscribers as are too remote to be able to comply with this request, may expect that we shall take the most expeditious method of recovering such arrears. We have adopted this resolution with reluctance, but are determined to adhere to it, as the only mode, since frequent remonstrance's have been found unavailing, of doing ourselves justice. From those who are sufficiently near to deliver us Produce in Washington, we ready to receive the following articles at cash prices, viz. Well cured Bacon Flour, Indian Meal, Corn, Tallow, Sugar and country Linen, at any time before the said 21st day of July.

The Mirror, Washington Kentucky   The Eagle, Maysville, Kentucky

Gentleman holding subscription papers for publishing A Report of Debates and proceedings in the approaching Convention, are earnestly requested to return them as soon as possible to Hunter and Beaumont, in *Washington and Frankfort*

Taken up by John Mahan living on the waters of *Mill creek*, and posted with Richard Tilton a justice of the peace for the county of *Fleming*, on the 24th of April, 1799 A BROWN MARE four years old this spring, supposed to have suckled a Colt last season, fourteen hands high, branded on the near shoulder with (W. H.) and on the rear buttock with   valued at 18 £ by John Mahan and Nathaniel Fitch Teste Richard Tilton June 11th 1799

Twenty Dollars Reward. Stolen out of his range about 12 miles below *Col. Rankin's Mill*, and on the road leading from thence to *Newtown*, on Sunday the 16th A BLACK HORSE, six years old this spring, fourteen and a half hands high, light made and active, has a small star in his forehead inclining to the left side, both hind feet white, with a remarkable black spot about the size of a round ninepence in the white of his near hindfoot, a switch tail, and no brand. He was stolen off by a certain Robert Barker of *Mason County*, a man about 30 years old, near six feet high, dark complexion, and weighs probably near two hundred, had on a brown linen shirt & overalls, and a striped linsey jacket of crossways. He also carried off a new man's Saddle, double skirted with a guilted hog's skin seat, neatly made. Whoever secures the said Horse and Man so that I get the Horse, and the Thief be brought to justice, shall receive the above reward, or ten dollars for the thief alone. Teste George B. Thomson Bracken, June 19th 1799

Six Dollars Reward. Runaway from the subscriber living on the road leading from *Charlestown* to *Washington*, a likely NEGRO MAN named *BILLY*; about five feet eight inches high, twenty six years of age, of a pleasing countenance, had on when he went away a pair of leather overalls, short linen coat and a pair of boots, no hat on; he can change his dress when he pleases. Any person taking up said Negro and delivering him to me shall receive the above reward and all reasonable charges paid by me. Rawleigh Chinn. June 10th 1799

The Washington Troop, Are desired to attend at their usual parade ground, in full uniform, on the 4th of July , at 11 o'clock. John Brown, Capt.

Ten Dollars Reward.   STOLEN LAST NIGHT out of the enclosure adjacent my dwelling house, A BLACK HORSE, about eight years old -

The Mirror, Washington Kentucky The Eagle, Maysville, Kentucky

something better than 14 hands high- both hind feet white - paces or canters in preference to any other gait - has on his back a small hurt by the saddle. For the Horse, and Thief brought to justice, I will give the above reward and three dollars for the Horse only. W. H. Beaumont

Notice. Is hereby given, that on Monday the first day of July, that I shall proceed to take the depositions of sundry witnesses to establish the beginning of an entry in the name of John Tabb, in Bourbon county, and on the waters of Hinkston, that calls for two ash Saplins growing from one root; with the letter K marked on each of them, and standing at the fork of a branch and on the East side thereof, and four or five miles nearly North East of Harrod's lick and do such other acts as the Commissioners may think proper, and agreeable to law. Philemon Thomas.

I will sell a prime tract of land, of three hundred acres, on Cabin Creek, including the forks; on which are about one hundred & fifty acres excellent bottom. The whole will be disposed of, together or in parts, to suit those who may wish to purchase, and a general warrantee deed given. For particulars respecting the terms, apply to me in Mason County. Charles Pelham.

To all whom it may concern. Take notice, that the purchasers under the preemption of Philip Pendleton Asse. Of Wm. M'Cleary', will attend at his improvement on the North Fork of Licking above the mouth of Pharo's Creek with commissioners appointed by the county court of Mason, on the first day of July next, then and there to take depositions for perpetuating testimony respecting the said improvement and boundaries, and to do such other things as the law directs. Archibald Wiggins

The subscriber is now opening for sale, a handsome assortment of Dry Goods, Groceries, Hard Ware & Pewter, at his Mills, lately known by Wood's Mountpleasant Mills, two miles from Limestone; which he is determined to sell low for cash, and will take for Dry Goods and Hard ware, corn, Bacon Country Linen, Wheat & Tobacco. John Edwards. Sen..

To all whom it may concern. Take notice that I shall attend on Tuesday the 9th of July, with commissioners appointed by the Worshipful Court of Fleming County at the improvement of John Jones on Fleming Creek, to take depositions for establishing the said improvement and special cases of John Jones' preemption, and do such farther and other things as may be necessary under the law. William Kennan, party concerned in said claim.

The Mirror, Washington Kentucky   The Eagle, Maysville, Kentucky

Lands for sale in the state of Kentucky. David Barber

A Tavern. I wish to inform my friends and the public in general, that I have opened a public House in the town of Chilicotha N.W. Territory, the sign of the Red Lyon, Water Street. And have it in my power to accommodate travelers with any necessary they may stand in need of on the most reasonable terms. I always keep on hand a supply of Corn Oats & Hay. Good stabling and pasturage; supply travelers that are going through the wilderness with suitable provisions, & c. to carry with them and shall make it my study to merit the approbation of those who will please to favor me with their custom. William Keys.

Mason County, April Term 1799. Meeker & Cochran, of the house and firm of Meeker Cochran & Co. against James and William Armstrong. It appearing to the satisfaction of this court that the defendant William Armstrong, is not an inhabitant of this Commonwealth; and he not appearing to answer the complainant's bill agreeable to law and the rules of this court upon the motion of the complainants, by their attorney, it is ordered that he appear here at the next August Court on the first day thereof in person or by some attorney of said court and answer the said bill, or the same shall be taken as confessed, and it is further ordered that a copy of this order be inserted in the Mirror, two months successively, another posted at the door of the Court House in mason county, and that this order be published some Sunday, at the door of the Baptist Meeting House in Washington. Test, Thomas Marshall Jun. C.M.C.

Mason County, March Term 1799. Robert B. Morton, against Bertrand & J. Ewell, C. Pelham, Wm. Wood & Rawleigh Chinn. It appearing to the satisfaction of this court that Bertrand and Jesse Ewell are not inhabitants of this commonwealth, and they having failed to enter their appearance agreeable to law and the rules of this court; upon the motion of the complainant by his attorney, it is ordered that unless they do appear here in the first day of the next August court, in person, or by some attorney of said court, and answer the said complainant bill, the same will be taken as confessed, and it is further ordered that a copy of this order be advertised in the Mirror, two months successively, and another posted at the Baptist Meeting House, in Washington some Sunday immediately after divine service and a third at the door of the Court House in said town. Teste, Thomas Marshall, Jun. C.M.C.

Friday, July 5th 1799

The Mirror, Washington Kentucky   The Eagle, Maysville, Kentucky

Cincinnati, June 18. By a letter received in this town last week, from a gentleman at Natchez, dated 4th May, we are informed, that the Indians had, a few days prior to the above date, stabbed a white man in the streets of that town. No mention is made in the letter, what induced the Indian to commit this act. It mentions that the people in that quarter seem very apprehensive of danger from the Indians - and they by no means think it safe to travel, at present, through the Wilderness.

We find it necessary to intimate to all persons indebted to the office of the Mirror for subscription, advertising or otherwise, that payment is expected to be made prior to the twenty-first day of July next. All who are at that time, more than six months in arrears, except such of our subscribers as are too remote to be able to comply with this request may expect that we shall take the most expeditious method of recovering such arrears. We have adopted this resolution with reluctance, and are determined to adhere it as the only mode, since frequent remonstrance have been found unavailing, of doing ourselves justice. From those who are sufficiently near to deliver as produce in Washington, we are ready to receive the following articles at cash prices viz. Well cured Bacon; Flour, Indian Meal, Corn, Tallow, sugar and country Linen at any time before the said 21st day of July. Mir. Edit.

State of Kentucky, June term 1799. Washington District. Thomas Bodley, James Hughes, Robert Pogue & Robert Campbell, against John Taylor. The defendant not having entered his appearance agreeable to an Act of Assembly and the rules in this Court and it appearing satisfactorily to the Court that he is not an inhabitant of this commonwealth, on the motion of the complainant by his attorney, it is ordered that he appear here on the third day of the next November Term and answer the complainant's bill, and that a copy of this order be inserted for two months successively in the Mirror, another posted at the door of the Court House in Mason County, and that this order be published some Sunday immediately after divine service at the door of the Baptist Meeting House in Washington. Teste, Francis Taylor, C.W.D.C.

State of Kentucky, June Term 1799. Washington District, Thomas Bodley, against Abraham Drake, Samuel Meredith, & George Clymer defendants. The defendants not having entered their appearance agreeably to an Act of Assembly and the rules of this Court and it appearing to the satisfaction of the Court that said defendants Samuel Meredith and George Clymer are not inhabitants of this commonwealth; On the motion of the complainant by

The Mirror, Washington Kentucky   The Eagle, Maysville, Kentucky

his Attorney, it is ordered that the said defendants appear here on the third day of the next November Term and answer the complainants bill, that a copy of this order be inserted for two months successively in the Mirror, another posted at the door of the Court House in Mason County, and that this order be published some Sunday immediately after divine service at the door of the Baptist Meeting House in Washington. Teste, Francis Taylor, C.W.D.C.

State of Kentucky June Term 1799. Washington District. Henry Lee against Charles Morgan, William Ward and others. It appearing that the order for publication had herein, at the last Term was never executed; and it still appearing satisfactorily to the Court that the said Charles Morgan is no inhabitant of this Commonwealth, on the motion of the complainant it is ordered that the said defendant Charles Morgan appear here on the third day of our next November Term and answer the complainant's bill that a copy of this order be inserted for two months successively in the Mirror, another posted at the door of the Court House in Mason County, and that this order be published some Sunday immediately after divine service at the door of the Baptist Meeting House in Washington. Teste, Francis Taylor, C.W.D.C.

State of Kentucky June Term 1799. Washington District. Thomas Bodley, James Hughes & others against Charles & Eli Metcalfe, Lewis Craig & John Walden. The defendant John Walden not having entered his appearance agreeably to an Act of Assembly and the rules of this court and the court being satisfied that he is not an inhabitant of this Commonwealth. On the motion of the complainants by their attorney, it is ordered that he appear here on the third day of our next November Term and answer the complainant's bill, that a copy of this order be inserted for two months successively in the Mirror, another posted at the door of the Court House in Mason County, and that this order be published some Sunday immediately after divine service at the door of the Baptist Meeting House in Washington. Teste, Francis Taylor, C.W.D.C.

Strayed from the subscriber the 2nd of May last a gray horse 20 years old no brand or mark perceivable, also one iron gray mare 4 years old this spring branded thus (2) on the near shoulder and buttock, the mare had on a small bell fastened with a leather strap and small iron buckle both in good order any person delivering the above creatures or either of them to me in Fleming county 4 miles from Flemingsburgh or giving information; shall be handsomely rewarded for the same. Wiliam Quantance.(sic)

The Mirror, Washington Kentucky   The Eagle, Maysville, Kentucky

Notice. On October next, application will be made to the County Court of Mason for an order to Establish a Town on the waters of Cabin Creek, near the mouth of the Little East Fork of said Creek, on the land of the subscriber and on a claim entered in the name of Joseph Delana; the Court will also be requested to appoint Trustees for that purpose   Hen. Disbrow

Taken up by John Mahan living on the waters of Mill Creek, and posted with Richard Tilton a justice of the peace for the county of Fleming on the 24th of April, 1799. A brown mare, four years old this spring, supposed to have suckled a colt last season, fourteen hands high, branded on the near shoulder with (W.H.) and on the near buttock with   valued at L 18 by John Mahan and Nathaniel Fitch. Teste Richard Tilton.

I will sell a prime tract of land Of three hundred acres, on Cabin Creek, including the forks, on which are about one hundred & fifty acres excellent bottom. The whole will be disposed of, together or in part to suit those who may wish to purchase and a general warrantee deed given. For particulars respecting the terms, apply to me in Mason County.   Charles Pelham

To all whom it may concern. Take notice, that I shall attend on Tuesday the 9th of July, with commissioners appointed by the Worshipful Court of Fleming County, at the improvement of John Jones on Fleming Creek, to take depositions for establishing the said improvement and special cases of John Jones' preemption, and do such farther and other things as may be necessary under the law. William Kennan, party concerned in said claim.

Errata. In the two last lines of George H. Thompson's advertisement, in the last page of this paper, instead of "Ten Dollars for the thief along," read "Ten Dollars for the horse alone."

Wednesday July 10th 1799

A gentleman from Chilicotha, informs us, that so far from the Indians in that vicinity having any hostile intentions toward us, they shew every disposition to cultivate a good understanding. Some of their young men had been in the habit of taking off horses from the frontier settlers those have been carefully sought after and restored by the other Indians, with a promise to do everything possible to prevent similar depredations.

The Mirror, Washington Kentucky   The Eagle, Maysville, Kentucky

Ten Dollars Reward Stolen last night out of the enclosure adjacent my dwelling house, a Black Horse, about eight years old - something better than 14 hands high - both hind feet white - paces or canters in preference to any other gait - has on his back a small hurt by the saddle. For the horse, and thief brought to justice, I will give the above reward and three dollars for the hose only. W. H. Beaumont

Twenty Dollars Reward. Stolen out of his range about 12 miles below Col. Rankin's Mill, and on the road leading from thence to Newtown, on Sunday the 16th inst. A black horse, six years old this spring, fourteen and a half hands high, light made and active, has a small star in his forehead inclining to the left side, both hind feet white, with a remarkable black spot about the size of a round ninepence in the white of his near hindfoot, a switch tail, and no brand. He was stolen off by a certain Robert Barker of Mason County, a man about 30 years old, near six feet high, dark complexion, and weighs probably near two hundred, had on a brown linen shirt & overalls, and a striped linsey jacket crossways. He also carried off a new man's Saddle, double skirted with a guilted hog's skin seat, neatly made. Whoever secures the said horse in Mason that I get the horse and the thief be brought to justice, shall receive the above reward, or ten dollars for the thief alone. Teste, George B. Thompson. Bracken.

The Mirror, Washington, July 17, By request. In Commemoration of American Independence in Winchester, Clarke County, on the 4th of July 1799, at the house of Edmund Callaway, the following toast were drank by an assembly of the inhabitants of the said town and its vicinity vix. 1st. The Day, and those who honor it. 2nd The Constitution of the United States. 3rd. The Congress of the United States. 4th The Militia; may they be the supporters of the American Laws, and a terror to its enemies. 5th The Guillotine; may it appear in America, and be exercised when tyrants and sycophants invade the rights of freemen. 6th May American Patriotism in an early time, revenge all insults on freedom by any corrupt administration. 7th. The friends of good Government, Law, Liberty and Order. 8th The people of the United States; may they exercise their privileges as their duty requires. 9th. Republicanism; the basis of good government, and emblem of the rights of Man. 10th Peace with honor, and a friendly commerce with all nations. 11th. May the state of Kentucky support her dignity as an independent branch of the union. 12th. Opposition to, and revenge on all invasions of the rights of freemen, whether foreign or domestic. 13th. The state of Kentucky; may the socially and peaceably participate in the reciprocal advantages resulting from a free navigation of the River

The Mirror, Washington Kentucky   The Eagle, Maysville, Kentucky

Mississippi. 14th A good free and equal constitution for the state we live in. 15th. May the Ministers delegated to France, by their instructions influence and exertions, restore an honorable peace between the United States and that Republic. 16th Low Salaries, Small taxes, an Universal Peace, and an everlasting plenty. After which, in peace and order, the company retired to their respective abodes.

Fleming County. Taken up by Samuel M'Coy, living in Fleming County on Fleming Creek. An Iron Gray Horse, three years old, fourteen hands high ... appraised to ƒ8 Before William K?? Joshua Stockton.C.T.C.C.

The Subscriber is now opening for sale, a handsome assortment of Dry goods, groceries, Hard Ware, Pewter, in Washington, in part of .the house occupied by Mr. James Dobyns which he is determined to sell low for cash, and will take for dry goods and hard ware, corn, bacon, country linen, wheat and tobacco. John Edwards. Sen.

Letters remaining in the Post office, Washington Kentucky, July 17th 1799. John M'Adow, William Ashly, *Bracken County*. Asael Broohover, Grier Brown, Lewis Bullock, Samuel Berry, *Bracken County*, John Beasley, Esq. *Manchester* 2. Samuel Broadwell, *near Riddles Mill*, Major Robert Beals, *at the mouth of the Scioto*; Robert Brackenridge, *Esq. Near Mays Lick*; Adam Bravard, Benjamin Beall, Esq. Barney Cararan, care of Mr. Jamerson, *Millersbourgh*, Col. John Crane, *Adams County N.W.T.* 2. Edward Collins, Andrew Cochran, Rebecca Caldwell, Henry Chapman, William M'Clean, care of Mr. M'Dowell, James Currey, 2, Carral Combest, Robert M'Connell, William Clayton, Acquila Cord, 2, Jacob Combelt, 3. James M'Clune, Michael Cassiday, Esq. Thomas Chain, James M'Cartty Soloman Dill, Charles Dale, *Bracken County*. Col. John Edwards, John Elder, John Eldridge. Robert Findley 3, Elijah Freeman care of Nathaniel Shaw. Major John Findley, *Upper Blue Lick*, Hugh Fulton, Esq. Ezekiel Forentan Doctor William Goforth, Mr. Grainger, John Graves, *mouth of Paint Creek*, N.W.T.,.. William Gardner, care of Abner Overfield. Mashack Hunt, William Hedleston, 2, Samuel Hedges, 2, John How, George Hamilton, care of Daniel Vertner, James Handy, Joseph Hunter, Richard Harker, *Indian Creek*, William Hanna, *Bracken County*, Capt. Heth, Jonathan Henderson, Michael Hofman, *Germantown*, George Hamilton, *Cynthiana*; John Hanson. Ignatius Jones, Aron Johnsen, *Mays Lick;* William Judd son of Wm. Anthony Johnson, William Jones. John Keith, Thomas Keith, John Kennedy, James Key. Peter Light, *Limestone*, Robert Leake, *12 miles from Washington*. Timothy Mayhall,

The Mirror, Washington Kentucky   The Eagle, Maysville, Kentucky

Limestone; Thomas Marshall, Jun. *Clerk of Mason County,* 2. Henry Massey, Esq. 2, Mr. Metcalf, John Malone, Nathaniel Massey, Esq. Mary Moore, *care of* Abner Overfield, Zorababel Maddox, John Mullanphy, *care of* John Taylor, *Limestone,* James Morrison, *Adams County, care of* Joseph Kerr Esq. Major Lewis Moore, 3. Mr. Nickols, Jenny M'Namar. Abner Overfield. Nathaniel Patterson, *Bracken*, 2, John Pickett, Col. Alexander Parker, 3, Edward Payne, Esq. William Robinson, Martha M. Rice, Jane Rogers, William Reed, *near Rankins Mill;* James Robinson Garrards, *Lancater Town.* Aaron Stratton, 2, Richard Soward, *Sheriff of Mason*, 2, Leah Selley, Mr. Shotwell, Rebekah Stephenson, *Little Bracken*; Joseph Stephenson, James Sanders, James Sargent, *Hamilton County N.W.T.* Richard Tilton, Mr. Taylor, *Limestone*, Frank Taylor, Francis Taylor, Jacob Boon or John Taylor, *Limestone*, Stephen Treacle. Alexander Verner, *near the three Islands.* Thomas Worthington, 3, Capt. William West, John Walton, *Bracken County,* Revd. William Wood 3, Abraham William Wells, Esq. William Washington, Robert Wilson, *Limestone.*

Notice That there will be a petition presented to the next General Assembly for the division of the counties of Bourbon, Mason, and Fleming, for forming a new county on Main Licking.

Twenty Dollars Reward. Run away from the Subscribers living in Scott County, Kentucky, on the 4th of July, two Negro men, one a Mulatto by the name of Major, about 5 feet 8 or 9 inches high, 24 years old; hath a piece out of the left side of his nose; a tooth out before; Cloaths unknown. Also a black fellow by the name of Phill, perhaps he will call his name Phill Burley; hath a scar on the little left finger; nearly the same height and age, but larger made; took with him a Cashmere Coat, with a split on the left shoulder 5 or 6 inches long; Several kinds of good cloaths. Any person that will take up the said slaves, and confine them in any Jail in Kentucky so that the subscribers get them again, shall receive the above Reward, & if brought home, reasonable expenses. John Sutton, William Sutton.

Whereas, I purchased from John Stewart, a certain quantity of land lying in Campbell county (now named Pendleton) in Kentucky State, and gave said Stewart my obligation for five pounds nineteen shillings (it being balance to him coming) payable, I think, on the first day of September in the year 1799, and there has other claims come against said land, to which said Stewart was knowing before said sale. It appears to me that it was an intended fraud of said Stewart, he now being determined to leave said state - therefore I forewarn all persons from taking assignment on said obligation

The Mirror, Washington Kentucky   The Eagle, Maysville, Kentucky

as I am determined not to pay it unless compelled by law.   John Stewart, Jun.

Wheat Wanted.   We wish to purchase a few hundred bushels of merchantable wheat delivered at Orr's Mill near the mouth of Lawrence's Creek, any time in the Months of October and November next. We have on hand a quantity of flaxseed Oil in good painted barrels which we will sell low for cash also a handsome assortment of large and small castings, Iron & Steel, warranted good, & a small quantity of Lead, Spanish Indigo and Window Glass, which we will either sell by Wholesale or Retail on the most moderate terms. As we intend setting out for Philadelphia next month, we must once more request those indebted to us either by Bond, Note or Book account, to make payment on or before the 20th of August next, on failure they may depend on suits being brought without either respect to persons or sums.   Morrison & Vertner

Wednesday July 24th 1799.

Domestic Intelligence.   Lancaster, June 29th.   On Wednesday last Lieut. Howard of the United States troops in consequence of some offensive words which appeared in the Reading Eagle, printed by Mr. Schneider, determined to take satisfaction by an appeal in the cowskin, by some mistake or disappointment, Lieut. Howard instead of meeting with Mr. Schneider, met with his journeyman whom he immediately began to whip, before the door of Judge Rush. A crowd instantly collected and young Mr. Heister and other interfered. In this situation the officer drew his sword on the most active, which was Heister. The latter retired a few paces and seized a Garden Hoe, with which he struck the armed of the officer in so a violent a manner as to break and lacerate it to a dangerous degree. Judge Rush then inter.. Lieut. Howard was bound in heavy recognizance.

Washington, July 24.   For the Mirror, Messrs. Hunter & Beaumont. Gentlemen, To rescue innocence from the opprobrium of malicious insinuations must ever be a pleasing talk to the benevolent soul. With this view we request you to give the following incident which occurred here last week a place in the Mirror. On the evening of Saturday the 29th ult. A traveler, who called himself Hedges, and said he lived at Wheeling, came to Mr. Benjamin Urmston's tavern keeper in this place, and put up for the night.   He pretended he was in great hurry to get to Millersburgh in Kentucky where he was to receive a sum of money, and must start early the next morning: Yet notwithstanding his seeming urgency, he staid all the

25

The Mirror, Washington Kentucky   The Eagle, Maysville, Kentucky

next day, on the following morning (Monday) he rose very early and telling another traveler, who was rising at the same time to pursue his journey, that he would go to the sable and see how his horse was treated went out; and leaving his horse, saddle and bridle, without farther ceremony went on his way. Mr. Urmston, not knowing of his guest departure and supposing him to be some where in town, made no inquiry after him until dinner; and then finding no one knew any thing of him, concluded he must have gone to visit some friend or relation in the country; never supposing he would leave his horse and pursue his journey on foot. H remained under the influence of this conjecture for some days, when, the stranger not appearing, he became uneasy and began to inquire earnestly after him, but to no purpose, he could get no information of him. On Saturday, the news began to circulate through town; and by the next day, malevolence had forged a very suspicious tale much to the injury of Mr. Urmston's reputation, viz. "That a traveler riding an elegant horse, had put up at his house on Saturday week - that he went to bed that night and was not heard of since." Insinuating that Mr. Urmston must have been accessory to his sudden disappearance. The tale circulated until Monday, darkening as it went, when Captain Nathan Reeves, from the crossing of Paint Creek, came to town and developed the mystery. He informed Mr. Urmston and others, "That Hedges whom he had formerly knew, had called at his house on the day he should have disappeared from Chillicothe and took dinner with him - that he told him he was on his way to Cincinnati, and had left his horse sick at Mr. Urmston's." Thus, first has a circumstance, ludicrous in its nature, become through misrepresentation and a false gloss, an envenomed shaft to wound the reputation of a reputable citizen. We are happy to have in our p..., through the medium of your paper to place the affair in its true light. We are, Gentlemen, Your humble Servants, E. Langham. Sam. Finley. Chillicothe, July 8th, 1799.

A Speech spoken by the Chiefs of the Shawnanee Nation, at the Ottoway town, June 23rd 1799. To be delivered by Mr. Daconigait, to Col. Ward and Major Kenton living on Mud River. Brothers. We are very sorry to hear that you are distrusted by some of our young men, which is pointedly against out wishes, you may depend it is done without our knowledge. I mean, in regard to horses which might have been lost or otherwise taken. We have done our best endeavor to prevent such unjust conduct, and likewise to collect them, together to speak to them, but it is out of our power to get them all together as we find they know themselves guilty. As we cannot have any objection therefore against your inflicting any punishment that the defaulter may have been guilty of, such as those who

The Mirror, Washington Kentucky   The Eagle, Maysville, Kentucky

may be detected, please let us know of it before any punishment is inflicted, for this reason, we would wish to know who they are, we will be then able to judge and know how to treat those ill deserving men. Some of those fellows have come in, and we have taken the horses and they had in possession on supposition of their having been stolen or taken unjustly and we have sent them by two of our Chiefs, to our Father, the Great Chief at Cincinnati. Brothers, we are very sorry for what has happened by those bad men, and hope you will not blame us their superiors. May the Great Spirit above, unite and join hands together as brothers that they may never be teperated nor that the Tomohock may never be raised against our brothers as long as we may live. Brothers We hope you will make all your good neighbors aquatinted with our wishes, truth in God to keep with us for evermore. We are with hand and heart your Brothers. Nasawashigaw or Big Thigh. Makateywekashaw or Black Hoof. In presence of James Leath, Frederick Fisher

Whereas my wife Ellinner has absented herself from my bed and board and entirely withdrawn herself from my protection without cause or provocation. This, therefore, is to forewarn all persons from trusting or harboring her on my account, as I am determined to pay no debts of her contracting from this date. Hazzen Rollf. Mason County..

State of Kentucky, Washington District. June Term 1799. Thomas Waring against William Wood. Defendant. The defendant not having entered his appearance agreeably to an Act of Assembly and the rules of this court, and it appearing tot he satisfaction of the court that he is not an inhabitant of this commonwealth; on the motion of the complainant by his attorney it is ordered that the defendant appear here on the third day of the next November term and answer the complainant's bill, and that a copy of this order be inserted in the Mirror, for two months successively, another posted at the door of the Court House of Mason County, and that this order be published some Sunday immediately after divine service a the door of the Baptist Meeting House in Washington. Francis Taylor, C.W.D.C.

Debates in Convention. Very few copies of the subscription papers for report of the debates and proceedings in Convention, have been returned to me, I am under the necessity of soliciting those who have them in possession to transmit them without delay, as I can, at present form no idea whether it will be prudent to engage in the proposed undertaking. The friends to the publications it is hoped will renew their exertions in its favor,

The Mirror, Washington Kentucky   The Eagle, Maysville, Kentucky

as the expense, attending it cannot be defrayed without a very considerable addition to the present number of subscribers. Harry Toulmin.

Taken up May 9th by the subscriber living on Johnson's Fork of Licking, a Mouse colored mare, thought to be eleven or twelve years old, much saddle marked, about fourteen hands high, branded on the near shoulder (x) supposed to be done with the pot-hooks, and on the near buttock, (s) no other distinguishing mark. Valued to nine pounds. William Nudegate. Mason County ff. The above is a true copy from my Records. David Ballingal

Fleming County. Taken up by Samuel M'Coy living on Fleming County on Fleming Creek, an Iron Gray horse, three years old, fourteen hands high, branded thus (s) appraised to $f8$. Before William Kennan Esquire. Joshua Stockton, C.F.C.C.

Wednesday August 7th 1799. Extract of three letters from a Robert Liston (British Minister at Philadelphia) to President Russel (A Canadian Judge) It states to the British government of Canada, that in the event of that British province being attacked by any foreign power, the government of the United States Stood Pledged to supply a military force adequate to the exigency to defend that Colony, and to preserve it to the British Government.

Observations of the Editor. The originals of the foregoing documents, have been transmitted officially to the first magistrate of the union, several days back. The public however are entitled to an examination of matters in which they only are the persons really and critically interested. They were seized on a horse stealer of the name of Sweezy in Bucks County in this state. Sweezy had been one of the gang connected with the notorious Dones and Sinclair, the two former of whom were hanged in this state, and Sinclair after being acquitted in this State through an error in the indictment, was subsequently hanged in J????y. Sweezy was outlawed and fled to Nova Scotia and Canada, from the government of which latter colony he was sent to this city, with dispatches and on his return with the above document, was pursued under the former outlaw. He has escaped but his character called for an examination of a parcel which he left behind, in which these documents were found along with a great number of letters from certain old Tories resident in this state, to others who took refuge from justice in Canada. The papers were forwarded by the magistrate into whose hands they had fallen, to an officer of this state government, by

The Mirror, Washington Kentucky   The Eagle, Maysville, Kentucky

whom they were forwarded to the President of the United States. Such is the history of the detection of those papers. Upon their contents there is room and occasion for a wide and serious train of reflections.

Notice is hereby given. To all persons who are indebted to the subscriber, to come forward and settle off their accounts, for that it will enable him to discharge those debts of his contracting. Those who neglect this notice may depend upon being dealt with according as the law directs. He has now also on hand a variety of men's and woman's saddles, bridles and harnesses of all sorts which he will sell on moderate terms for cash, wheat, corn, oats or beef cattle. N.B. Old work repaired with the quickest dispatch and on the most moderate terms. By the public's humble servant Samuel Lucas. Washington.

For Sale, For Cash, Ninety four acres and quarter of land lying on the Cross Roads where Brook's road crosses the road leading from Washington to the Salt Licks. Charles Pelham. Mason County.

Wednesday August 14th 1799.

Unfavorable accounts have been several days in circulation respecting the dangerous situation of the Miami settlements. It seems, the surveyor, out running lines, consonant to the treaty of Greenville, has been forbidden to proceed by a considerable party of Indians. The settlers on Mad River, have taken the alarm and are fortifying themselves particulars, we have not been able to learn . A few days, we presume will give us to know how far these reports are founded on reality. Tho there is little reason to doubt that the inhabitants are under considerable agitation. The British minister's letters to his Canadian Correspondent, by the Horse Stealing Envoy, S- (Sweezy) inform us, that the Indians have applied for an alteration in the boundaries stipulated in the treaty made at Greenville, and have been refused- this is probably the ostensible case of the present dissatisfaction of the Indians - the real one may be better known to the British agents & emissaries, scattered so profusely over the United States.

We have since heard that the Indians have appeared in a considerable body on horseback - that they declared themselves to have peaceable intentions towards the people of the United States, and avowed their determination of attacking the Chickasaws, who had intruded on their hunting grounds. Their having sent away their women, a circumstance unusual, when they war only with one another, as has been the occasion of so much alarm

The Mirror, Washington Kentucky The Eagle, Maysville, Kentucky

among the frontier settlers, and affords a good reason to doubt the truth of their professions.

Whereas my wife Elizabeth and me have separated by mutual consent, this it to forewarn all persons from trusting her on my account, as I am resolved not to pay any debts of her contracting unless she returns to my bed and board as usual. Given under my hand this 12th day of August 1799. William Craig.

Strays. Taken up by Benjamin Blackburn, living in Montgomery County on Flat Creek, one sorrel horse, about eight years old this spring, about fifteen hands high, had on a three shilling bell marked thus X, no brands to be seen. The said horse is a natural trotter. Appraised to 18 pounds. Given under my hand this 14th day of June, 1799. David Hughes

Taken up on my plantation on Hingston, between the mouth of Somerset and Bane's Creek, a bay horse, ten years old, about fourteen hands one inch high, has a small star in his forehead, some saddle marks, had on a small bell with a hole in the upper end of it, marked on its four side S.M. tied on with a rope; had on three shoes. Edmund Baxter, Bourbon County, April 22d. 1799

Segars for sale. I wish to inform my friends and the public in general, that I have on hand, in the house formerly occupied by Mr. Machir, nearly opposite the Court House, a large quantity of Excellent Segars, which I will sell on the most reasonable terms by retail, and make a considerable allowance to those who purchase by wholesale, to sell again. And also Tallow-Candles, of the best quality may be had as above. Peter Brough. Washington. August 13th 1799.

Take Notice, that whereas I gave a bond, in the year one thousand seven hundred and eighty two to William Parker, penalty of 1 500 conditioned to convey to said Parker, a certain tract of land, containing four hundred and fifty acres, on Stony Creek, a branch of Wataga River, then in the state of North Carolina (now perhaps Tennessee). Which said tract of land, the said Parker has never paid for agreeable to his contract; and the underwritten then being a minor, or under age, and incapable therefore to transact such business, is determined never to convey the said land to the said Parker nor his heirs or assigns. And I do hereby forewarn all persons from ? assignment on said bond. John Robinson, Junr. Harrison County Kentucky July 25, 1799.

The Mirror, Washington Kentucky   The Eagle, Maysville, Kentucky

To all whom it may concern. Take notice that the purchaser under the preemption of Terrel, and Hawkins assignee of John Fitzpatrick, will attend at his improvement with commissioners appointed by the county clerk of Mason, on the thirtieth day of this instant, August, then and there to take depositions for perpetuating testimony respecting the said improvement and to do such other things as the law directs. Joseph Desha. August 6, 1799.

Will be offered for sale to the highest bidder, for cash, on Friday the 23d and Saturday the 24th inst. At Jacob Thomas's, Washington, nine in lots, containing four and a half acres; and seven out lots containing thirty five acres, with all the improvements on said lotts, taken as the property of John Johnson, to satisfy an execution of Alexander Macgregor against said Johnson and George Wood. James Dobyns, S.M.C. a copy test, Macgregor. N.B. If the property does not sell for cash, at three fourths of the value it will be sold at three months credit. Macgregor.

Look this way! Ran away or decoyed off from the subscriber living in Clark County, on July 15th 1799. A likely Negro man, by the name of Louis, about 18 or 19 years old, of a low stature, but well fet; of a dark complexion, with a small darker spot of a small size on one of his cheeks; his dress I am not certain of, Is believed he had on when he went away, a dark stripped coat, and waistcoat with large red spots and linen overalls. Whoever takes up this fellow and secured him so that I get him, shall received twenty dollars I taken within the state, if our of the state, fifty dollars reward and all reasonable charges paid. William Bronaugh. August 14th 1799.

Ten Dollars Reward. Ran away from the subscriber living near Mays Lick, on the first of March last, a Negro Woman named Mary, about twenty five years old - very black and stout made - a large scar over her left eye - her clothing cannot be described. The above mentioned reward will be given to any person delivering her to the subscriber, or to Mr. Thomas Williams in Washington. Jonathan Stout. Mason County, August 12, 1799.

A most extraordinary transaction took place a few days ago at Bristel in Pennsylvania - a recruiting party of the standing army is stationed there, consisting of nine or ten persons including the Captain. One of the recruits, named Adam Frazer, had been charged with absence from roll call, a few minutes after the appointed time. The captain ordered him into an oven where he detained him four hours, and from whence the unfortunate victim

The Mirror, Washington Kentucky The Eagle, Maysville, Kentucky

of military despotism was taken in convulsions! When this detestable transaction was first communicated tot he Editor, he could not credit it; but upon a minute inquiry on the spot finds it to be too well authenticated to be deemed or questioned. We improve and progress towards Turkish and Russian affinities very rapidly. Aurora.

Notice. On November next application will be made to the County Court of Fleming for an order to annex one hundred acres of Land to the town of Flemingsburgh, lying adjacent to said town - it being part of a tract of Land entered in the name of Benjamin Roberts. George Stocton, Jun. August 2d, 1799.

Wednesday August 21st, 1799.

Several anxious inquiries having been made concerning the Editor yesterday - and as he could not attend to them all and perform his duty at the same time - he is induced to satisfy them and inform the readers of the Aurora generally in this manner - that the Editor was yesterday between nine and ten o'clock arrested by John Nicholas, esq. Marshal of this district, upon a warrant from Judge Peters and on behalf of the administration, for publishing in the Aurora of the 24th instant, a certain matters alleged to be defamatory or untrue concerning the administration. By the marshal, he was treated in a gentlemanly manner - and by Judge Peters, he was very politely allowed until Friday morning to bring forward securities. To those who are personally acquainted with the Editor, no declarations concerning his past or future conduct are necessary - to those who know him only as the organ of public sentiment - a trustee, for the public to detect and expose public errors, and to promote the public good - he can give only these brief and steadfast assurances, that he has not published a fact which he cannot prove, and that neither persecution nor any other peril to which bad men may expose him, can make him swerve from the cause of republicanism - or prove himself unworthy to be the successor of the defendant of Franklin, in whose steps it is his pride and pleasure to tread with the same confidence in his country and the law. Aurora.

Washington, August 21. Letter from Col. William Ward, one of the principal settlers on Mad River, to the Editors. Gentlemen, Since there is so great a rumor thro' the country respecting an Indian War, it might perhaps be gratifying to the public to hear the circumstances that gave rise to the report, from one who has seen and heard the matter investigated

The Mirror, Washington Kentucky   The Eagle, Maysville, Kentucky

between the Whites and Indians. It appear the Indians were calling in their scattered people, for the purpose of settling them in some regular manner, as they were before their dispersion by the wars. About the same time some ill disposed persons informed the Shawanee Indians that the Chickasaws were about making war against them, and that some of them were then laying in wait to put their hostile designs in execution. At this the Shawanees were much alarmed and made preparations for their defense, from which preparations (and by exaggerated accounts of them too) the Whites took alarm, thinking that the Indians intended war against them, which caused some persons, whose situation exposed them to the most danger, to go in search of the truth, and by bringing the parties together, discovered (in my opinion) that the apprehension of a war between them was wholly groundless, and that some evil minded or imprudent persons, had brought things to the pass they were, through design or folly. I have in my possession the chief of the correspondence on the subject; but as it is lengthy, I don't suppose it worth your trouble to print, or the people to read it; assuring you and them, that what I write is all that can be got out of it, I was present at the investigation of the whole affair. William Ward. Col. Ward is just come in, and traveled as far as Cincinnati, with four Shawanee Chiefs, whose design is to explain the matter to the Governor of the N.W.T. Col. W. has left his family behind him, and is entirely void of any apprehension of danger. The Indians having vacated a small town where they had crops of corn growing, was the chief cause of alarm. The reasons for leaving it, have been satisfactorily explained.

On Tuesday last two men were found murdered about 60 miles from Chillicothe, on the road leading from thence to Muskingum River; one of them is said to be a Major John M'Farlin, of Cheat, a branch of the Monongahela. The bodies were shot through in several places, dragged some distance from the place where they were killed, and thrown into a run; one of their horses was killed and scalped. Some accounts say, there was a third person also found dead at a considerable distance from the others.

Since hearing the above we have been informed, that two white men are apprehended on suspicion of being the perpetrators of this horrid outrage.

Will be sold for cash on Monday the 26th day of this instant, being Court day, one still, taken from the revenue due the United States by James Scott, - and one still taken for revenue due by John Taylor, to the United States, and one still, taken from Robert Criswell, for revenue due the United States. Lewis Moore, Col. Revenue.

The Mirror, Washington Kentucky   The Eagle, Maysville, Kentucky

Notice. I will attend on Monday the 26th day of this instant, being Court day, in Washington, and at September Court in Fleming and Bracken, to take the entries of riding Carriages. The Distillers will please to meet me at the same time and place to pay their revenue - the law will be put in for e against all delinquents. Lewis Moore, Col. Revenue

Taken up by Nathan Rawlings, one Strawberry Roan Mare, seven years old, fourteen & a half hands high, a wart under its right eye, had on a small bell. Said Rawlings lives on Richland Creek, in Harrison County. The Mare is appraised to ten pounds.

Wednesday August 28th 1799.

A Full page letter written by Arthur O'Connor who was in Kilmainham Prison in 1799 in England. The article mentions also a Mr. M'Nevin. Both O'Connor and M'Nevin were Irish and were given the option of leaving country, never to return, if they signed a declaration.

Frankfort, August 15. The trial of Henry Field of Woodford county, for the murder of his wife, came on last Monday week, before the District Court in this town. Greater anxiety in the spectators, who were very numerous, we have seldom seen, than was exhibited upon this occasion. The horrid circumstances attending the atrocious act - the respectable character which the accused had supported, til this lamentable event took place - and the known abilities of the Counsel engaged on both sides - all contributed to exercise a degree of interest in the event of the trial which has seldom been equaled. It continued the whole of the week, and the unhappy man received sentence of death on Monday last. He is ordered for execution on the 19th of next month.

The supposed murderers of the late Mr. Langford, (Micaijah Harp and Wiley Harp, who a short time since broke out of Danville jail) we are sorry to learn have added to the black catalogue of their crimes. Authentic information has been received that on the 22d of July, they killed William Ballard, in Knox county, State of Tennessee; and on the 23d, Isaac Coffe (Cosse?). On the 19th they killed James Brazel, near Wolf River in Cumberland Mountain, and on the 31st murdered John Tully in Stockton Valley - They were seen the 2nd of this instant on Marrowbone, a north branch of Cumberland River. We are happy to hear they are closely

The Mirror, Washington Kentucky The Eagle, Maysville, Kentucky

pursued, and sincerely hope they will ere long meet the punishment which the atrocity of their crimes demand.

Cincinnati, August 20. It is with great pleasure we inform the public that a principal chief of the Shawnees and three others, came to this place on Friday last, and have given assurances to the Governor, that their nation, and as far as they know, all the others are perfectly friendly to the Americans. That the frontier having been evacuated by them, and the people drawn together to build forts, had distressed them & added to the alarm they were under about the Chickasaws, who as they had been informed were coming in great Force to attack them. That the being in arms at their towns was with no other view than to defend themselves against the Chickasaws, and that they had brought their women and children into them, and were making some fortification about them for their security. That the sole and of their coming here at this time was, that the people might be satisfied they had no bad design against them, and that Neinimsic another chief well known to them, had gone to the Great Miami, to give the people the same assurances.

Hark!! Six dollars reward. Broke or stolen out of the pasture of Captain Daniel Morris on the old Lees town road, seven miles from Lexington, on the night of the 18th instant, from the subscriber living on the road leading from Washington to Lee's Creek, Mason County, four miles from the River Ohio, one Bay Horse, two years old last May, near or about fifteen hands high, well made, has a blaze in his forehead which makes a point to his left eye, his mane hangs on both sides of his neck has been decked this spring, part of his near hind foot white above the footlock. It is probable he is not stolen or stopped he will make for Mason county where he was raised. Whoever takes up said Horse, and the Thief apprehended, shall have the above reward, and reasonable charges paid, for the horse only three dollars will be given. John Hopkins. Mason, County.

Valuable Military Lands for sale. On the Little Miami & Todd's Fork, and on Paint Creek near the Falls. Col. Alexander D. Orr near Limestone, is authorized to sell the former and John Brown, Esq. At the Falls of Paint Creek the latter. S.T. Mason

The subscriber wishes to lease his Grist Mill on the North fork of Elkhorn for a term of years; this Mill has an extensive custom, with two pair of stones in good repair; he will also rent the plantation whereon he did live adjoining said Mill or a like term of years, this place as a public stand is

The Mirror, Washington Kentucky   The Eagle, Maysville, Kentucky

equal to any in the country the house, well suited for that purpose, the farm contains about 80 acres of cleared land, ten acres in good grass and clover, ten in Timothy Meadow, the balance plow land in good repair; on this farm stands a barn 60 by 20 feet, good stables and other out houses; a good still house with two good stills and every apparatus for working them. This place will be rented altogether or separate, provided the whole shall be taken - apply to the subscriber one mile from the mill on the road from George Town to Paris. William Henry. Scott County   N.B. There are houses on the above farm sufficient to accommodate several families. .

August 7, Extract of a letter from a gentleman in Coneca, 256 miles from Mississippi, to his friend in Wilmington, N.C. dated May 23rd 1799. "At a meeting lately held at this place, with the Creek Indians, they have allowed an escort of two chiefs and 20 warriors, to ensure the safety of the party who are running the boundary line between the United States and Spain, in the Indian Territory, which will be completed in three months."

A very extraordinary phenomenon has lately appeared in the vicinity of Palatine, on the Mohawk river of an epidemic distemper amongst the wild pigeons. Strong evidences, it is said, on dissection have been discovered of a morbid affection in the throats of these animals, and a very general apprehension has prevailed among the inhabitants, from some instances of persons being afflicted with the malignant sore throat who had improvidently fed on the flesh of the diseased birds.

Notice. As I intend setting out for Philadelphia next month, we request all those indebted to us either by bond or book account, to come forward and make payment by the twentieth of this month as no further indulgence can be given. William Cleneay. Washington.

Cheap Bargains. To be sold that large and valuable plantation in Bullitt County, on which the subscriber now lives; containing 1200 acres of land, 160 acres of which are cleared; the improvements are valuable, during and convenient viz. One stone dwelling house, 28 feet by 22, three stories high; one Log ditto, two stories, 30 feet by 20, having a cellar under the whole; a good barn, 90 feet by 38, three stories high, with stone stabling, 12 feet high under the whole of it; an Orchard of 400 bearing Apple trees, and sundry other usual improvements, too numerous to mention. There is near the house an excellent spring of water, and the premises lie convenient to navigation, being only four miles distant, and Bullitt's Lick six. The subscriber will also sell for cash or Negroes, all the residue of the land he

The Mirror, Washington Kentucky   The Eagle, Maysville, Kentucky

possesses in the state; and if the above should not meet with purchasers, he will offer for sale, one fourth of Cumberland Iron Works. As it is presumed no person will purchase the said property without viewing it first, further particulars are unnecessary. Persons moving to the Green River Country are informed, that Pot Metal of different dimensions from the Cumberland Furnace, may constantly be had at their respective Court Houses. Adam Shepherd.

September 18, 1799 From the last Nashville paper, Second Convention of Bees. To complete the phenomenon that took place last years, those animals are now paying their annual visit to the place. On Sunday last one swarm appeared at Bellview, the seat of Judge M'Nairy, and pitched on a small tree in the yard; and on Monday four, one of which wished to make a stand in the balcony - attempts have in vain been made, to accommodate them with hives; but this favor they will be no means accept. They continue to occupy their first position, and will probably increase to the number of last year, which was 48 swarms.

Omitted last week for want of room. The yellow fever has again made its appearance in New York and Philadelphia, the interments on the 22nd ultimo, in the latter city amounted to 11 grown persons and eight children.

The last Cincinnati paper says, that Major Ludlow has completed the Indian boundary line without the least hindrance or inconvenience from the Indians and had returned to that place.

Adam Frazer, the soldier that was baked at Bristol, it seems has deserted; it is remarked that had he remained five minutes longer in the oven, he had never violated the laws of war in this manner – which plainly proves that too much lenity was shewn him.

John Armstrong, respectfully informs the public and his friends in particular that he has just arrived from Philadelphia with a neat and general assortment of merchandise, well chosen for the person and approaching season, consisting of dry goods, hard ware, queen's ware & groceries, which he will sell low for cash, or such produce as will suit his market. Limestone, Sept 10th 1799.

Fifteen pence reward. Run away from the subscriber living in Washington Kentucky, a well grown boy for his age; He is supposed to be about nineteen years old, and six feet high. Any person that brings him to my

The Mirror, Washington Kentucky   The Eagle, Maysville, Kentucky

shop and delivers him to me shall receive the above reward. William Ginnings. August 21 1799

The subscriber passed a bond to William Pearle Jun. Of Kentucky on or about the 13th of September 179? for one hundred pounds Virginia Currency, for the residue of the payment for two hundred acres of land in the same state, and part of a larger tract and being informed that the said William Pearle refuses to lay the same off in an equitable manner and agreeable to the spirit and meaning of the contract made with him, he hereby forewarns all persons not to take an assignment of the said bond, as he is determined not to pay it until the said land is properly laid off and conveyed, or until the said William Pearle shall agree to submit the location to some different persons. William Dibell. Farquire County, Virginia, June 18th 1799.

I wish to sell 7000 acres of land in Pendleton County, lying between Ohio and Licking, near the mouth of the North Fork adjoining M'Cartys on the poll road from Washington to Cincinnati. The survey is divided into 14 lots of 500 acres each. I will give one, two or three years credit to purchasers, on particular conditions and take Negros, Horses or produce in payment. The land is on of a good quality for small grain, near navigation, and the title indisputable. Also 4000 acres of land in the neighborhood of where I live together with a Grist and Saw Mill which will be disposed of on the above terms. John Grant. Campbell County, August 1799.

Taken up by Benjamin Woffor, (Wossor?) living near the Miami road, one light bay mare, five or six years old, fourteen hands and one inch high, natural paper, black roam and tail, and black list on her back, had on a good five shilling bell a leather strap and single buckle. Appraised to eighteen pounds before me. William Woodward.

Take Notice That the underwritten gave his bond unto a certain John Robinson, Senr. Dated the 22nd day of April 1799, for three hundred dollars, payable the first day of October next, in consideration for a tract of Land to contain one hundred Acres. But finding that the aforesaid quantity is not within the limits specified in his bond to me, I am determined not to pay the aforesaid three hundred dollars, nor any part thereof until the quantity of one hundred acres is laid off and deeded to me, agreeable to contract with Robinson. And do hereby forewarn any person from taking any assignment of said Bond, as I am determined not to pay the money. Mason Johnston. August 30th 1799

The Mirror, Washington Kentucky   The Eagle, Maysville, Kentucky

Hog's Bristles wanted. Cash will be given for a quantity of clean hog's bristles by Christian Willmann. Washington September 6th 1799.

A journeyman baker wanted. Generous wages will be given by the subscriber, to a young man acquainted with the baking business, who can come well recommended. Richard Ross. Washington, Sept. 16th 1799.

C. Freeman, physician & surgeon; Respectfully informs his friends and the public that he has returned from the Indian towns from the Northwestern territory with a fresh supply of different kinds of herbs, roots, plants &c. used in the healing art. He continues (with the blessings of God) to perform cures in a easy safe and expeditious manner, without the least injury to the constitution. Viz:- Fevers, inflammations, eruptions, hemorrhages, fluxes, fits, cramps, convulsions, head ache, sore eyes, bleeding at the nose, colds, coughs, pain the breath, spitting of blood, pains in the stomach, indigestion, night sweats, inward debilities, low spirits, vapors in men, hysterics in women, difficulty in making water, bloody urine, constiveness and rheumatism, effectually destroys worms, cures fits and wandering pains arising in different parts of the body, the effects of the improper se of mercury, green wounds, old sores, ulcers, burns, scalds, cancers, scald heads in children piles & fistulas, the whites in women and all feminal weaknesses in both sexes & all venomous bits effectually cured. The many cures performed within four years past, which will fully appear (to any gentleman who will please to call upon him, being too lengthy for this paper) by papers and vouchers of cures performed, now in his hands properly attested, and whose authenticity cannot be denied. N.B. He has taken a large commodious house on high street, in a healthy part of the town, for the reception of persons who are affected with diseases, (and reside at a distance) they must find their own bedding. Such as may think proper to put themselves under his care, may depend on the greatest attention being paid to them in the faithful discharge of his duty, and the most reasonable charges. None need apply unless they have money or property to pay or the medicine received or can give approved security payable in four months. Lexington,

Washington, September 25th. Henry Field, who was sometime since found guilty of the murder of his wife, was executed at Frankfort on Thursday last in pursuance of his sentence.

The Mirror, Washington Kentucky   The Eagle, Maysville, Kentucky

Mason County, August Court 1799. Simon Kenton, against Jonathan Rumford & John Dougherty defendants. This day came the complainant by his attorney and it appearing to this court that the order made here in at the last term was not executed, and that the defendant Dougherty, is not an inhabitant of this state, & he not appearing agreeable tot he rules of this court, it is ordered that he appear on the first day of the next November term in person or by attorney and answer the bill of the complainant & it is further ordered that a copy of this order be published in the Mirror for two months successively that another Order be posted at the door of the Court House in Washington and a third be posted at the door of the Baptist Meeting house some Sunday immediately after divine service. Teste, Thomas Marshal, Junr. C.M.C.

The subscriber being desirous of removing into the country, is disposed to sell his property in Millersburgh; a part in cash, and a plantation with indisputable title, will be received in payment. They consist, viz. Of a saw mill in good order. Two lots, a log-house, a kitchen, smoke house, garden and large out lot, improved in meadows and an orchard. One lot with a log house and stone chimney. One lot with a frame house and brick chimney. 2 Lots with a large log house and stone chimney, kitchen & c. convenient for a tavern. 1 Our lot improved in meadow, at the proximity of this last lot. J. Savary

Three Dollars Reward. Lost on Monday the 9th of this instant, on the Lexington road near the Bridge of the North Fork of Licking, a Red Morocco Pocket Book, containing a number of Executions, Notes of hand and other papers which can be of no use to any person but the proprietor. Any person producing the book and papers, to the subscriber, shall have the above reward. Edward Dobyns, D.S.M.C. Washington, Sept. 15th 1799. .

Ten Cents Reward. Ran away from the subscribers, living in Washington on the 15th July, an apprentice boy named James Whitaker. Whoever takes up said boy and delivers him to us shall have the above reward. Samuel & James Baldwin. Washington, Sept. 25th 1799

Taken up By Henry Foley, one sorrel mare, about six years old with a star, no brand to be seen; with an old bell, a leather collar and buckle; about thirteen hands high appraised to eight pounds. One Bay horse colt, with a star and snip about two years old last spring. Appraised to four pounds ten shillings by Samuel Powel & Robert Smith. January 10th 1799

The Mirror, Washington Kentucky   The Eagle, Maysville, Kentucky

Twenty Dollars Reward. Ran away from the subscriber living in Campbell County Kentucky, on the 15th instant, two Negro Men, one about 22 years of age, named Bob, about five feet ten inches high, slender made, with a very pleasant countenance, tolerable handsome, no particular marks only a large scar on the right knee occasioned by a burn last winter, which causes him to limp a little, had on when he went away a shirt and overalls of six hundred linen, a gray cloath great coat, a felt hat & a buff cashmere vest. The other is a thick heavy fellow, named Charles about twenty years old and about six feet nine inches high with uncommon thick heavy feet, a smiling countenance, thick bushy wool on his head, a small scar on one of his thumbs occasioned by a burn when young, had on a tow shirt & overalls, a striped swansdown vest, a short brown coat of lastick cloath somewhat worn, a felt hat, and blue spotted silk handkerchief round his neck. I expect they will change their names; I also expect they have procured a pass and will attempt to go to some distant parts. The above reward & all reasonable charges will be given if delivered to me or secured in Jail in the United States, or ten Dollars for either. Sq. Grant. September 20, 1799

Notice. The first day of October next, being a General Muster Day. The Washington Troop, are desired to meet in full uniform at their usual parade ground, at the hour of nine a.m.. John Brown, Capt. September 25th, 1799.

Whereas I purchased a tract of land of Josephus Walters of Mason County Kentucky which said tract lies on the Ohio river, in the N.W.T. adjoining Walters's ferry, for which I have paid him a considerable sum, and there yet remains apparently due on my bond 109 dollars - whereas the said Walters has not made a title to said land in pursuance of our agreement, this is to notify that I shall not pay, the said sum of 109 dollars until obliged thereto by due course of law. Cain M'Kinney. N.W.T. September 20th 1799.

October 9, 1799. For Sale, a likely Negroe Woman, who is a good house servant, together with her child, about three years old - For terms, apply to the Editors of the Mirror

1500 Dollars. Was delivered to the Post Master. Here in the post office on the evening of Tuesday the 17th past, a letter directed to Mr. John Miles, merchant in Baltimore, containing two Alexandria bank notes, No. 4320, favor or William Taylor, and dated 30th April 1798, for one thousand dollars, and No. 4511 favor of John Pleasants, and dated 10th December

The Mirror, Washington Kentucky   The Eagle, Maysville, Kentucky

1798, for five hundred dollars; which letter has been suppressed in a post office and the bank notes taken out, as the public mail was neither stopped, molested nor robbed. Bankers and merchants are particularly requested to watch the circulation of said notes and stop them: and any person giving such information as will lead us to our money shall have five hundred dollars reward, and no questions asked.   Wilson & Swann. Fredericksburgh, Virginia, 9th September 1799.

Dancing School. The subscriber, having taught with great reputation, in different parts of Pennsylvania and Virginia, last Winter and Spring, and whose letters of introduction to this place and Lexington are most respectable; begs leave to inform the ladies and gentlemen of Washington and its vicinity, that is honored with their patronage, he intends opening a school here as soon as a sufficient number (sixteen or more scholars) shall subscribe. He teaches particularly, the Minuet, Cotillion, Cotillion, French & English sets, in all their various and ornamental branches - exclusive of which, he teaches the most fashionable country dances and the City-Cotillion, taught in New York, Philadelphia and Baltimore. His terms are three dollars entrance, and five at the expiration of the quarter. R. Haughton. Washington, Oct 9th 1799.

Whereas my wife Kisziah Smith, for reasons only known to herself, refuses to live with me, and we have agreed to part - I do hereby forewarn all people from dealing with her or trusting her, the said Kisziah Smith on my account, as I will pay or be answerable for any of her dealings. Witness my hand. William Smith, Bourbon County, October 9th 1799.

Notice. All persons indebted to me are requested to come forward immediately and either discharge their accounts or give notes for the balance due. Such as do not pay the necessary attention to this advertisement, will undoubtedly have suits commenced against them, for the recovery of their respective debts. J.P. Duval. Mason County, October 9th, 1799.

Twenty Dollars Reward. Ran away from the subscriber living on Greer's Creek, within two miles of Versailles, in September ninety eight, about the twentieth day, A Negroe Woman, called Allice, about thirty five years of age a middle-sized woman, passes for a free woman, and an artful sensible wench, and full of artifice, and should any person apprehend the said wench & bring her to me, he shall be entitled to twenty dollars. For securing her in any jail in this state or any other, so that the owner may get

The Mirror, Washington Kentucky   The Eagle, Maysville, Kentucky

her again shall receive the sum of ten dollars. Rowland Hughs. October 1st. 1799

Letters remaining in the post office Washington Kentucky, October 1st, 1799. Achsa Anderson, *near Mill's Station*, Henry Ardreett, Richard Applegate, Thos. Addison, *at Mr. Mayo's, Newport.* John Baddolet, Millersburgh, D.Blandchard, James Buchanan, *near Blue Lick*, Rudolph Black, *Germantown* 2, David Brodrick, Andrew Badgley, *Mayslick*, Joseph Brown, James Brown, John Baker, *mouth Little Bracken*, James Bailey, *Mays Lick.* Samuel Crane, junr. *Care of James Crane*, James Campbell, *Mays Lick*, Samuel M'Cartty *on the road between Washington and mouth of Licking,* Eli Collins, *Adams County*, Richard Compton, Robert Coleman, Betsey M'Connel, *care Basil Burgess*, James M'Coy, James Campbell, *care of James Wilson Esq.* Joseph Clark, *eighteen miles below Limestone, N.W.T.* John Cooper, *four miles from Washington*, James Currey, *near Nichols's Mill*,2. Charles Dale, *Bracken County*, Elmore Doggott, *Williamsburg*, Margaret Dye, Doctor Michael Dougharty , Revd. John E .Findley, Capt. John French. Robert Grayfor, Cornelius Gater, 2. Michael Hasman, *Germantown*, Thomas or Wm. Haynes, John Haller, Nathan Hill, George Hamilton, *Cynthiana*, Samuel P. Hedges, Owen Humphreys, *Keith's Mill,* Joseph Hancock, *Wm. Brookes's landing*, Notely Hays, David Henry. David Johnson, *Preston.* John Kenton, William Kennedy, Joseph Kerr. Gen. Lee, 2, Asa Lewis, John Logan, John Lewis. Edmund Martin, *Post Master Limestone* 2, Zorabable Maddox, 2, John Mullanphy, Alexander K. Marshall, Major Lewis Moore, James Morrison, *Adam County, N.W.T.* Thomas Marshall. Major Vall Peers, James Patterson, *care of Philemon Thomas*, George Philips, *near Limestone*, 2, Robert Poage, *Mays Lick*, 2, John Patton, Robert Powers, Ezekiel Pralston *on the Ohio.* Adam Ritchey, Ezekiel Ralston, *care of Andrew Alison, three Islands*, 2, Jonathan Ralston, *Manchester, N.W.T.* Robert Rachford *Millersburgh.* John Barrett, *Sheriff Adams County N.W.T.* 2, David Sharp, Lucas Sullivant 5, John Scot, *Millersburgh.* John Taylor 2, William Thompson *Cabin Creek, care of Hugh Hanna,* Nicholas Talirerro, *Bracken County*, John Thompson 2, Francis Taylor, Esq. Mr. Tom, *care of Mr. Hadon, Clarks Mill.* Richard Williams, William Wallace, Josephus Walters, Abram Williams, John Whittercher, *Licking,* John Waller, Esq. Millersburgh.

Advertisement. On the 25th of April last, was committed to the jail of this county, a runaway Negro man, who calls himself Thomas Smith, and says he belongs to one Valentine Peers, of prince William County, in Virginia,

The Mirror, Washington Kentucky   The Eagle, Maysville, Kentucky

and that he left his master on his way to Kentucky. Said Negro is about five feet six or eight inches high; his clothing, when committed, was green cloath breeches; a coat of the same kind of stuff, his jacket of scarlet cloath; and old wool hat; and old shoes and stockings. His master is hereby desired to come forward, prove property, pay charges and take him away. Nathan Williams Jailer. Westmoreland Jail, July 19, 1799.

Land for sale. Two thousand acres - one thousand of which is situated on Pepee Creek, and one thousand on a small creek, about two or three miles nearer to Chillicothe. These lands are of an excellent quality, and the title indisputable, the whole being surveyed upon Virginia military Warrants. A warrantee will be given, and patent procured. For terms inquire of Wm. M. Beaumont, Washington or George Mitchel Esq. Limestone.

For Sale. Several small tracts of land North West of the Ohio, and convenient Tanyard at Cincinnati; also a Plantation within four miles of Flemingsburgh, and one within six miles of Washington which I will dispose of on reasonable terms. I will give one hundred acres of land North West of the Ohio, to any person who will clear fifteen and erect a couple of cabins on a tract of Land of mine near this place. John Machir. September 28th 1799.

Ten Cents Reward. Ran away from the subscriber living in the town of Washington, on the nineteenth day of April last. An apprentice boy named Samuel Parent, aged about nineteen years, a thick well fet lad about 5 feet 8 or 9 inches high, with dark short hair. All persons are cautioned against harboring or dealing with him, and whoever returns him to me shall be entitled to the above reward. Joseph Brown. Washington, October 2nd 1799.

Wednesday October 16th 1799.

Domestic Extract from a letter from Chester County, dated September 14. Scarcely any of the late measure of government or the agents of it, have excited so much pain, animosity and alarm in my breast as the late trial of Jonathan Robbins, methinks I see him at this moment expiring on a gibbet, exhibiting to the world an evidence of the humiliated state of the American government - to the British nation an encouraging example to the continue the violation of our neutral rights - and to the American seamen the awful lesson how little he has from the dignity the justice or humanity of the

The Mirror, Washington Kentucky The Eagle, Maysville, Kentucky

people's present servants to encourage him to trust himself under the American flag. .. the rest of the article is political

From the Salem Gezeette. Mr. Cushing, by giving the following protest a place in your useful paper, you will much oblige me. I should have published it immediately after an interview with the President but he advised me not to do it; until the business was in a proper train..... Your most humble servant, Ebenezer Giles.

Extract of the letter sworn before Joseph Wood, Esq. In Beverly, in said county of Essex, personally appeared before me, Ebenezer Giles, commander of the Schr. Betsey, of said Beverly and James Wilson mate and Allen Stickland & Joseph Patch, seamen, belonging to said Schr. That on the 27th day of April, 1799, at the Island of St. Vincents, at a place called Layou Bay, on said schooner, there waiting for his British Majesty's ship of war Daphne, to pass by ... They ordered the Betsey to bring to.... As she came along side, Captain Giles said to the officer on board the boat, my friend, I was very sorry to have seen you drop astern. He answered, you damn'd rascal, do not call me your friend. The captain of the Betsey then told him that he hoped he should not find him to be his enemy. ...The captain of the Betsy was insulting and abusive language and demanded of said Giles his instructions which were immediately delivered up to him. Immediately after he arrived on board, the said James Wilson, Allen Stickland, and Joseph patch saw two men on board of the said ship violently beat Capt. Giles, one of them with a large piece of rope, and the other with his fist, and continued so to do for the space of more than thirty minutes sometimes by the violence of the blows received he was struck down; and they soon after sent Capt. Giles on board the Betsey, who when he came along side was not able to stand or walk by reason of the barbarous treatment he received. They further testify and say that they took Captain Giles on board his schooner in the cabin and took off his jacket and found it much striped and torn by the force of the blows of the rope's end. That Captain Giles was not able for the term of four days at least to come on deck, or do his duty. This is a full page article that cannot be reproduced here. Any one interested in the full account should read the actual text.

The Trustees of Franklin Academy are requested to take notice that the fourth Monday in this month is the time appointed for a stated meeting. As business of consequence requires their attendance, it is hoped they will be

The Mirror, Washington Kentucky   The Eagle, Maysville, Kentucky

punctual in attending that day, at the Court House about one o'clock, p.m. R.W. Waring C.T.F.A. Washington October 14th 1799.

Ran Away from the subscriber about the first of June last a Negro man named Blage, about eighteen or twenty years of age, speaks bad French and broken English, fond of Liquor and very talkative. I expect he will attempt to pass as a freeman. I will give twenty dollars reward, if taken on the north west side of the Ohio, and ten dollars if taken on this side and brought home, besides what the law allows. John Allen. Paris, October 1st, 1799.

Mr. Haughton's Dance school commenced the 15th instant, at thirty days in the quarter - twice a day; in the Court House. Night school for gentlemen, from 7 o'clock to 9 at six dollars.

By an advertisement published last Tuesday by Messrs Wilson & Swann, it may be inferred that bank notes were delivered to me, to the amount of 1500 dollars, and the whole tenor of the advertisement seems to be an attempt to throw an obloquy on my character. The following statement of facts which I can support by testimony, will at once remove the impression of my receiving money, and their villainous attempt at calumniating my character by their unjust publication. Mr. Swann of the house of Wilson & Swann, came to the post office between the hours of 9 and 10 o'clock on the evening of the 27th ultimo when he delivered me a letter when I asked him if it was double? He replied "yes, it was," and I took it and put it in the mail in his presence, as he staid some considerable time after the delivery of the letter, and which mail was regularly put up with the others as usual, and sent from this office. How Messrs. Wilson and Swann came by their information, that the letter was suppressed and bank notes taken out, I leave the public to decide. William Wiatt. Fredericksburg, Sept 12, 1799

Domestic Intelligence. Alexandria, Sept. 28. Gen. Davie, one of the ministers appointed by the President to go to France, arrived in town last evening, and this morning proceeds tot he Northward to join his colleagues.

Baltimore, September 30. Fire! The city was yesterday alarmed with a fire which broke out between 4 and 5 o'clock, p.m. in a carpenters shop belonging to Mr. M'Conky, on Wing mill hill, at the corner of High & Pruit street continued. The fire was said to have been occasioned by a segar.

The Mirror, Washington Kentucky The Eagle, Maysville, Kentucky

Newark, October 1. Suffex County, September 21, 1799. We just learned that after battalion training was over yesterday in Krolton (?) a noted friend to order and good government, Brigadier General Hill first stabbed a Mr. Uriah Albertson with his sword, a little under the eye, of which he instantly expired. We are not able to relate with certainty what gave rife to such a horrid act; but are led to believe that the heat of argument or the politics of the day, together with some degree of inebriation has produced his atrocious deed. Mr. Albertson was a respectable citizen, and has left a widow and several small children to deplore his untimely end. We understand that a jury of inquest was immediately called, who brought in a verdict of willful murder, committed by said Mill.

Washington October 23. Jonathan Robbins, a native of Connecticut, who was convicted of being concerned in a mutiny on board the British frigate Hermone, by which he expected to regain that Liberty which he thought his Birthright, and of which he had been deprived by a British press gang; was executed at Jamaica on board the Acaste Frigate on the 10th of August last pursuant to the sentence of a court martial. Thus fell his unfortunate American citizen, among the Martyrs, but by no means the first one, to the implacable vengeance of the Britain - his death will remain a lasting monument of the efficacy if not the excellency of Jay's treaty.

Notice. I have for sale in Paris, Bourbon county, twelve or fifteen hundred pounds worth of good merchandise, pretty well assorted, with part of a brick bu9ilding, facing the public ground, for which I will take good Military land near the Ohio River, with a small part paid in Tobacco, any where on the Kentucky river, from Cleveland's landing to Frankfort, or at Limestone, paid by the first day of February next. I will receive wheat at my mills in Mason, one half paid in money, the other half in Merchandise, on the delivery. Those inclined to meet the proposals may bargain at any time with Mr. David S. Brodrick, my agent in Washington, who will agree on the terms of delivery and payment of money. My lower mill is in order for receiving 5,000 bushels of wheat, which will be ground with dispatch as soon as water comes, and bolted through superfine and fine cloths, which are of the best quality. Those who deliver wheat in the mill to be manufactured, are to remove it from the mill with the offall in order for room for others, as I mean to do business with dispatch. John Edwards Senr. Washington, October 15, 1799. N.B. I have also in Paris, Bourbon county, a dwelling house well finished with eight large rooms together with a commodious dwelling for a family, well calculated for a public house,

The Mirror, Washington Kentucky The Eagle, Maysville, Kentucky

with suitable ..For terms apply to my agent in Washington as above or to Mr. Amos Edwards in Paris. I.E. Senr.

October 30, 1799 Domestic Intelligence. Trial at Hartford Connecticut. September 30. On the 28th inst. The Circuit Court of the District of Connecticut finished their session in this town. Isaac Williams was tried before this, on an indictment for having on the 27th of February 1797, at Guadalope, accepted from the French Republic a commission and instructions to commit acts of hostility and violence against the King of Great Britain and his subjects, contrary to the twenty first article for the Treaty with the United States; the French republic being then at war with the King of Great Britain. And said king being then in amity with the United States. On the trial it was admitted on the part of Williams that he had committed the facts alleged against him in the indictment; but in his defense, he offered to prove that in the year 1792 he received for the consul general of the French Republic, a warrant appointing him a third Lieutenant on board the Jupiter, a French 74 gun ship, that pursuant to the appointment, he went on board the Jupiter, took the command to which he was appointed, which vessel soon after sailed for France, and arrived at Rochelort in France in the Autumn of the same year. That he was naturalized in the various bureaus in that place the same autumn renouncing his allegiance to all other countries, particularly to America. This article is too long to reproduce here. It ends with a guilty verdict and he was sentenced to pay a fine of 1000 dollars, and suffer four years imprisonment. He was charged with another crime and given the same sentence.

Mr. Holt, Editor and proprietor of the Bee, a republican printer in Connecticut, was summoned before the district court to answer for a publication upon the recruiting service. Sympathy for the inexperienced youths who where adventuring into war contrary tot he inclination of their parents and friends, in may places dictated that production.

Land for Sale. I am authorized by Capt. Alexander Fowler of Pennsylvania, to dispose of one thousand acres of land, either on Peepee Creek or on a creek three miles nearer to Chilecothe - theses lands were surveyed upon Virginia military warrants and are excellent in their quality. Also one thousand acres situated on the first bluff at the mouth of Tennessee, a very commanding situation; for terms apply to me in Lexington, I.S. Wills Esq. Chilocotha, George Mitchell Esq. Limestone, or W.H. Beaumont Washington. C.Tatham

The Mirror, Washington Kentucky The Eagle, Maysville, Kentucky

I will sell the tract of land I live on being on Floyd's fork, Jefferson county, containing four hundred acres cleared, well watered, convenient to mills, and the salt works. It is unnecessary to describe the quality of the land, as it is presumed no person will purchase until they see it. An indisputable title will be made. Wm.Garrard. August 15, 1799.

Taken up by Murdock Cooper. On Cabin Creek, a bay horse, 14 hands high, 1 inch high, 8 years old, branded on the near shoulder I.W. and on the near buttock with a crooked iron. His hind feet white, a small star in his forehead, has several saddle spots. Appraised to forty dollars. Posted before me. Winsloe Parker. Oct. 23, 1799

Eight Dollars Reward. Strayed or stolen from the pasture of Mersham Bett, Junr. In Fleming county on the 3rd day of this inst. A bright bay mare five years old last spring, 14 hands 3 inches high has the appearance of the pole evil, tho' never had it. Likewise the jaw on the near side appears to have been broke, marked with saddle spots, no other marks either natural or artificial that I recollect. Whoever brings said mare to the subscriber living in Flemingsburgh in the county aforesaid shall receive the above reward and all reasonable charges by Jacob Steele. Flemingsburgh, October 29t^h 1799. N.B. On the same evening that said mare was missed, was found int he pasture a strange mare, a bright bay about fourteen hands high judged to be eight or nine years old, appraised to 15 pounds. J. Steele.

Land for sale. Twenty thousand acres, lying on Eagle Creek, in the state of Kentucky. The survey is of an excellent quality, equal if not superior to any on the creek, and lies on the main road leading from Georgetown to Cincinnati. The subscriber will attend on the survey during all November. Mr. John Sterrit near Georgetown will inform of the particular place where he may be found. The title is looked on to be without dispute. A general warrantee will be given the land sold low and settlers meet with every encouragement. Horses will bet taken in payment. Thomas Potter. October 30th 1799

Two Dollars reward. Lost on the 19th or 20th of this instant a needle worked pocket book marked S.F. on the road leading from Chenoweth's station to Germantown, containing one note on John Ruth, payable to Thomas Lewis to the amount of L 40 given the 2nd day of June 1797 and payable the 2nd day of June 1799, with some other papers of small value.

The Mirror, Washington Kentucky   The Eagle, Maysville, Kentucky

Whoever find the said pocket book, and delivers it to me, shall have the above reward. Thomas Lewis. October 24th 1799.

Taken up by James Faris on the 2nd day of August 1799, a strawberry roan mare, 7 years old this spring branded S. on the near buttock valued to 12 L also one small year old sorrel colt with a small blaze in its face valued at L3.0.0 by William M'Cormick and William Dudley. Entered Record with Richard Tilton Justice of Fleming County. October 1st 1799 Washington, September 6th 1799.

Wednesday, November 6th 1799. Domestic Intelligence. Extract of a letter from John Kinnand, Kng of the Hitchitaw Tribe of Creek Indians to James Seagrove, Esqr. Dated in the Creek Nation, 22nd August, 1799. "At the time your talk came to me, there was great confusion in the towns below, nie about the running of the line, which was stopped for some time, and it was owing to Colonel Hawkins' never seeing the people or giving them any of his talk. The Indians stole a great many horses from the people at work, on the line, but they have now all agreed to the line being run according to your advice, and they have returned all that they stole. They came on with the line within twenty miles of the Fork of the Chatahouche and Flint River, where they were stopped two and a half moons, but have gone on now and go over Flint River. They made a mistake in setting their compass when they started from Conaco river, near Pensacola, and had to send back their captain* o take another start. I expected he has got back by this time and will go on with the line. They intended to start again with the line in sixteen days. They have great plenty of provisions in two vessels lying loaded at the forks of the Chatahouche and Flint river, which is but 80 miles from my house. I am very glad to tell you my friend that there is nothing now on the part of the Creek nation to hinder the line being run and completed. I have had no so much running about on this business and to put the Indians right by explaining your talk, that I am almost worn out with fatigue." We are informed that all the principal Chiefs of the Siminolias, and some Chiefs of the Lower Towns, on the Chatahouchee and Flint Rivers, are on their way to Colerain to consult with Mr. Seagrove, that on the 16th inst. Is appointed for their meeting at that place.
*Supposed to be one of the Surveyors, or perhaps Mr. Ellicott, the commissioner.

Extracts. From the Aurora. Robbins is no more, in vain he pleaded that he was an American, that he had been pressed by the British and that he was not concerned, in the murder of the infamous Pigot or his officers. All was

The Mirror, Washington Kentucky The Eagle, Maysville, Kentucky

in vain, British vengeance demanded his life, and he was delivered up to an ignominious death. But by whom?? All American know. Ill fated man to be born in this country! Had he been a Swede, a Dane, a Prussian or even a barbarous Russian, he would not have been pressed nor forced to serve where horrid oppression excited its sufferers to sacrifice the tyrants to a just indignation. The lamentable exit of that poor fellow is a tragedy, peculiarly affecting to every true American or genuine Republican. It forms a precedent of the most dangerous nature to the liberty and lives of all Americans. The worthy Judge Bee will not be quickly forgotten. His merits are duly appreciated and shone conspicuously on a late transaction. Let not any of the hardy sons of Columbia neglect to pray for him in their morning or evening orisons.

Notice On February next application will be made to the County Court of Fleming for an order to establish a Town on Big Sandy, on the land of the subscriber, and on a claim entered in the name of John Preston. The Court will also be requested to appoint Trustees for that purpose. James Harris. November 7th 1799.

Eight Dollars Reward. Run away from the subscriber, on the Sunday the 12th day of October, an apprentice boy, named James Wood. About 16 years of age, light complexion, Nearly 5 feet high and has remarkable white short hair; had on when he went away a green Elastick coat, black vest and tow cloth overalls and a wool hat. Whosoever takes up said apprentice and secures him so that I may get him again, shall have the above reward. Richard Compton. Mason County, October 23d.

November 20, 1799. Domestic Intelligence. Baltimore, October 17. The following invention of a gentleman in North Carolina, promises to be of much general utility. A Mr. Jones, a native of this state, has constructed a machine upon a plan, both simple and new, for the conveyance of water to any part of the house, and what renders the invention more surprising, water may be conveyed from a spring one hundred feet below the surface of the Earth. The expense of a machine of the greatest given power, will not cost more than twenty pounds. We hear Mr. Jones intends applying for a patent.

Philadelphia. October 31. About one o'clock on Tuesday morning a fire broke out in the Livery Stable of the late Mr. Martin Murray, situated on the corner of Moravian alley and Watkins court, which consumed the stables, together with 17 horses, a large number of valuable carriages,

The Mirror, Washington Kentucky   The Eagle, Maysville, Kentucky

harnesses &c. and extended with opposition to a number of adjoining buildings, the consuming situation of which precluded the proper sue of the engines. Before it yielded to the exertions for the citizens, above 15 dwellings houses and stores, were either totally destroyed or very materially injured. Those stores contained property to a considerable amount. The following are the principle losses which have been sustained by the fire. A stable the property and in the tenure of Mr. Michael Murray, where the fire originated. Seventeen horses, two carriages, nine chairs and seven sleighs, were consumed with this building. A dwelling house, the property and in the tenure of Mr. Michael Murry. A store the property and in the tenure of Mr. Walker containing a quantity of spirits, sugar and Molasses entirely consumed. Two dwelling houses the property of Mr. Walker. A dwelling house and shop in the tenure of Mr. Clayten, blacksmith. A stable with two brick tenements adjoining the property of Messrs. Wilcox. The brewhouse of Mr. Morris, and the sugar house of Mr. Muhlenberg, altho often imminent danger, were prevented by the active exertion of the Citizens, from receiving but little injury.

A political article on the case of Jonathan Robbins.

Washington, November 20. At the District Court now holding in this town - Robert Barker was yesterday found guilty of horse stealing & ___ ___. Cleveland acquitted, after having been arraigned for a similar offense.

Whereas my wife Elizabeth Comton has this day eloped from my bed and board, without any just cause by me given, these are for to forewarn all persons from crediting her on my account, as I am determined to pay no debts of her contracting - Given under my hand this 18th of November 1799. Jacob Comton.

Wednesday November 27th 1799. Washington, November 27. At the close of the District Court held in this town last week, Barker, the unfortunate man who was convicted of horse stealing, received sentence of death; his execution is appointed for the twenty eight of next month. Yesterday several Negroes were tried .. the court of quarter sessions two of whom were capitally convicted; viz. A woman for the murder of her child, and a man for burglary - another woman was also found guilty of larceny and one acquitted.

The Mirror, Washington Kentucky The Eagle, Maysville, Kentucky

The following incident has attracted much notice at Paris. Citoyen Felix, two years ago brought two Lions a male and a female to the National Menage. About the beginning of June, Felix fell ill and could no longer attend to lions. Another was forced to do his duty. The Lion sad and solitary remained from that moment constantly seated at the end of his cage and refused to receive anything from the stranger. His presence even was hateful to him, and he menaced him by bellowing. The company even of the female seemed to displease him, he paid no attention to her. The uneasiness of the animal afforded a belief that he was really ill, but no one dared to approach him. At length Felix got well and meaning to surprise the lion, he crawled softly to the cage and he wedge only his face against the bar, he patted him with his paws, licked his hands and face and trembled with pleasure. The female ran to him also, the lion drover her back, seemed angry and fearful that she should snatch any favors from Felix, a quarrel seemed to take place between them. He caressed them by turns. Felix is now seen in the midst of this formidable couple, whose power has settled & he holds a kind of conversation with them. If he wishes they should separate and retire each to their cages, he has only to speak a word, if he wishes that they should lay down to shew strangers their paws armed with terrible claws and their throats full of tremendous teeth - at the least sign from him they lay on their backs, hold up their paws one after another open their throats and as recompense, obtain the favor of licking his had. These two animals of a strong breed, are five years and a half old; they were both of the same mother, and have always lived together.

November 27th, 1799. Take Notice. Whereas my wife Betsy has left my bed and board without any just cause. I forewarn any person or persons from trusting her on my account, as I am determined to pay none of her contracts. Benjamin Van Amburgh. Mason County, Kentucky, November 1, 1799.

Wheat and flaxseed wanted. The subscribers will give merchandise for wheat delivered at Sloo's, Rankin's and Orr's Mills. Also wanted a few hundred bushels of Flaxseed delivered in Washington. S & D. Tebbs. November 20, 1799.

Whereas I gave a note to John M'Comas payable the 20th June 1800, for the sum of sixty pounds two shillings and six pence, in part pay for land purchased of him, and whereas he has not fulfilled his agreement with me with regard to said land, this is to forewarn any person from taking an

The Mirror, Washington Kentucky   The Eagle, Maysville, Kentucky

assignment on said note, as I am determined not to pay the same, until he complies with his agreement. Jonathan Rumford. November 26, 1799.

Having explored the United state's Military lands, I propose to locate warrants to the best advantage, on being allowed one eighth, and will attend on the land immediately after locating, and shew any section in which I may be employed. As not less than 4000 Acres can be registered, or located, I will receive any less quantity and class them with others so as to make up the necessary quantity. Warrants or letters addressed to me at Washington (Pen.) any time previous to the 17th December and on that day until the 21st day of February next, at Mr. Israel Isreal ..chestnut street Philadelphia, will be duly attended to. W. McCluney. November 15, 1799

Territory of the United States, North West of the River Ohio. Washington County, Whereas a writ of attachment hath issued from the court of common pleas of said county, directed to the Sheriff of said county returnable at December term 1799, at the suit of Perley Howe against the Lands, Tenements, goods, chattels, effects, rights and credits of Nathaniel Gardner Dabney, for fifty-six dollars and fifty cents - notice is therefore given to the said Nathaniel Gardner Dabney that unless he does appear and give Special bail to the said action, Judgment will be entered against him by default and the property attached disposed of as the law directs. By order of the court. Benjamin Ives Gilman, Prothonotary, Edwin Putnam, attorney for the Plaintiff, Marietta, October 30th 1799.

To all whom it may concern. Take notice, that I shall attend on Wednesday the 18th of December with commissioners appointed by the worshipful court of Mason county to perpetuate testimony in behalf of a preemption patented in the name of James Montgomery, deceased and do such things as the law may require. James Montgomery

Taken up by the subscriber in Fleming county on the waters of Johnson's Fork, one bay horse, about six or seven years old, branded on the near buttock. C, shod all round, a switch tail, about fifteen hands high appraised by Lucius Chapin and John Boyd to one hundred dollars. James Kellay.. October 31st 1799.

The Eagle, Maysville July 16, 1818
R. Crookshanks At two dollars and fifty cents pain within three months from the receipt of the first number, or three dollars at the expiration of the year or for 52 numbers.

The Mirror, Washington Kentucky   The Eagle, Maysville, Kentucky

Maysville, Kentucky. The enterprise and industry of the inhabitants of this town, having placed it in a remarkable flourishing situation, and the subscribers being proprietors of …. Have thought it admirable to add to its present consigned .. They have laid off into convenient streets and allies a sufficient quantity of land, situated in the bottom immediately above the said town, with a handsome situation from its extension. The advantages attending Maysville, more generally known by the name of Limestone, must be obvious to every man acquainted with the western country. It stands immediately on the bank of the Ohio, and is surrounded by a fine healthy, and fertile country on both sides of the river, and has been the deposit of the Merchandise imported from the Atlantic country for thirty years past. The main leading road from Philadelphia, Baltimore, and the eastern country generally, towards New Orleans, both by land and water passes this place and necessarily renders it interesting. The turnpike Road from the West makes it a point and if a rich country, and permanent establishments, can give a town importance this place must flourish. The subscribers offer their Lots on liberal terms, and will secure to the purchasers may privileges and advantages not common to others. The invite the attention of the Mechanic, the Manufacturer and merchant of the west under a full belief, that the advantages of all parties will be substantially prompted. The raw materials are abundant, capital and industry, with the first gifts of nature, must at this place ensure profit to correct enterprise. Any person wishing to purchase, can be accommodated on application to the subscribers. Samuel January, John Coburn, Maysville, or Limestone, KY. March 13, 1818

Tenders his services to the inhabitants of Maysville and its vicinity, as a practitioner of MEDICINE, SURGERY, &c., His show adjoins the drug store of J & Y. G. BYERS, near the market house. May 14, 1818   Dr. Orramel Johnston

Sale The subscribers tends laying off a town convenient streets and allies, at William B. Brooks' landing, on the Ohio river in Mason County, Ky. (to be named by the purchasers of Lots,) about three miles from Maysville. This place has many natural advantages of the highest importance. The landing is good, and the river hill of easy assent. There are excellent roads leading to different inland towns in the state. The surrounding country is healthy, fertile and thickly inhabited. The river bottom is wide and dry and the bank high and perfectly free from over-mowing. Kenady's Creek, which puts into the river at this place, affords and excellent Harbor for

The Mirror, Washington Kentucky   The Eagle, Maysville, Kentucky

Boats, equal to that at Maysville, and it is at least probable that assoc. as ware houses are erected and other conveniences to be had, that this place will have a share of the receiving and storing goods and shipping produce. The Lots will be laid off, and a public sale made, on the first Saturday in September next, when the terms will be made known, and attendance given by the subscriber living on the premises Richard Ritter. June 13, 1818 William B. Brooks Richard Ritter

Young Ladies Seminary. Mrs. SPENCER, Presents her acknowledgments to her friends, and informs them and the public that her school will commence the first Monday in June. TERMS OF TUITION A regular English course per qu'r 810.00 Reading, Writing and Needle work   6.00 Musick per annum 850, per qu'r 18.00 Drawing and painting per qu'r 8.00 Boarding $100 per anum, each young Lady to provide her own bed & c., and towels. Maysville, may 19, 1818

FAMOUS ANTIBILIOUS PILLS.THESE much esteemed Pills have been for many years prepared in Baltimore by the present proprietor, as may of our most respectable citizens can testy; and many of them have readily and gladly given certificates of their great value as a family physic. Lee's Antibilious Pills are, and have been for many years, sold and used as a family medicine in almost all parts of the United States and have always given general satisfaction; and their superior benefits are so highly esteemed; by a wise and deserving public, that they require no newspaper eulogy or puffs to recommend them. It is therefore only necessary to inform those that have been in the practice of purchasing Lee's Antibilious Pills, (and those who see a proper hereafter to vend them) that they put in wood boxes, with a bill of directions about them, that the plain outside wrapper contains, the words "Lee's Antibilious Pills," and on the other side, the proprietor's signature. - "Observe that none are genuine without the signature of Noah Ridgley (late Michael Lee & Co.") none other can possibly be received as Lee's Antibilious Pills. The proprietor most respectfully informs his friends and the public in general that he continues carefully to prepare (from the original receipts) Lee's ANTIBILIOUS PILLS, together with the whole of Lee's family medicines at his family medicine Dispensary, No 68, Hanover street, Baltimore - viz: LEE'S ANITBILIOUS PILLS, for the prevention and cure of Malignant, Bilious and other Fevers, admirable adapted to carry of superfluous bile, &c. &c. LEE'S WORM DESTROYING LOZENGES - certain and powerful remedy for destroying all kids of worms. LEE'S ELIXIR- a certain and effectual remedy for obstinate colds, coughs, weak stomachs & c &c

The Mirror, Washington Kentucky   The Eagle, Maysville, Kentucky

LEE'S GRAND RESTORATIVE AND NERVOUS CORDIAL a most valuable medicine for great and general debility, nervous disorders, loss of appetite &c. &c. LEE'S ESSENCE & EXTRACTS OF MUSTARD - an infallible remedy for sprains, bruises, rheumatism, numbness, chilblains &c &c LEE'S SOVEREIGN OINTMENT for the ITCH warranted to cure by only LEE'S AGUE AND FEVER DROPS, warranted to cure if taken according to the directions. LEE'S PERSIAN LOTION, for removing eruptions from the face, and curing tetters &c &c LEE'S INDIAN VEGETABLE SPECIFIC - a certain and effectual cure for venereal and gonorrhea, Lee's TOOTH POWDER which cleanses and beautifies the teeth. LEE'S EYE WATER - a certain cure for sore eyes. LEE'S CORN PLAISTER, for removing and destroying Corns LEE'S ANODYNE ELIZIRE, for the cure of head aches. The proprietor would be glad to insert the many certificates and letters recommending the above truly valuable medicines, but this in a newspaper, is impracticable - He therefore will increased confidence respectfully proffers them to a liberal and discerning public. DRUGGIST AND MERCHANTS are inform, that Lee's Antibilious Pills together with a general assortment of Lee's highly approved Family medicines can be purchased a the proprietor's Dispensary on the most favorable terms. They are very respectfully invited to call and convince themselves of the fact. They may be had on commission (where no agency now exists.) by giving approved references. They are sold by his appointments wholesale and retail by DAVID BYERS, Druggist Louisville, & J& E& G BYERS Maysville, who have just received a fresh supply from Baltimore. The above medicines are also sold by TILFORD, TROTTER & CO LEXINGTON and BUTLER & WOOD, Frankfort Kentucky And in almost all the principal cities and towns in the union. Please to observe that none can be Lee's Genuine Family Medicine without the signature of the proprietor, NOAH RIDGLY (late Michael Lee &Co.) April 24, 1818 Noah Ridgley

For Sale, 804 Acres of first rate land. The subscriber offers for sale 80 acres of excellent Land situate on the East Fort of Little Sandy, six miles from the mouth of Little Sandy, on which is a Grist and Saw Mill, newly erected, and four convenient dwelling houses and other improvements. There is a good proportion of bottom and up land. Any person wishing to make an advantageous purchase can have the whole (or to accommodate) one half of the above 804 acres on favorable terms, by making application to the subscriber on premises. James Johnson, Greenup C'y, KY June 5, 1818

The Mirror, Washington Kentucky   The Eagle, Maysville, Kentucky

LIST OF LETTERS
Remaining in the Post Office at Maysville, on the 1st day of July 1818 which if not taken out within three months will be sent to the General post office as dead letters.

A. Isaac Abbott, Richard Ailles, Wm Atkinson, Caleb Atherton,, Henry Arnold, John Armer 3

B. Umphrey Bell, Nicholas Barwell 2 Phantley R. Bean, Thomas Bear, Jinks Brown, Blacsslee Barnes, Ignatious Brawner, John Blanchard, William Butt, Thomas Briely 2, Edward Brewer, S.A. Bartram, Pleasant H. Baird, Purnel Brittingham, Benj. Bowman, Boas Broner

C. Lewis Craig, Evan Campbell, Robert A. Crain, Disa Claybrok, James Coulter, Thomas Clark, Robert Colberison, Thomas Carter, Ludwell Carye, Silas Caldwell, James C. Campbell, John Cochran, Wm. Cummings, William Campsey, Wm. Cordingley, John Coburn

D. James R. Duke 3 Abraham Depuy 2, John Davis, Jonathan Dart, Joseph Davis, Robert D. Dawson, Timothy Dennison, Anderson Donathan, James Davis, James Dillon, Henry Devour 2

E. Jesse Ellis, Duddley B. Ellis, Elizabeth Ellis, Resin Elliot, Lucinda Ellis 2 Chester English 2

F. Wm. Forwood, Jacob Fisher, James France, Susanna Fritter, John Farror, James Fullerton, James Ficklia, Hugh Fulton

G. Jesse M. Grant 2, Mr. Grayham, William Grayham, Samuel Gunsalus 2, Peter Gideon, Alex. Guthrie 2, Benj. B. Garnes, James Giant

H. Delana Holden, Samuel Helen, Richard Hammat, Philip Hawke, Aaron Hathaway, Woodruff Hoskins, Benj. Homes, Robert Hill, Washing. W. Hedges, Samuel Hopkins, Edward Holden,

J. Edward Jones, Mordica John, Edward O. Jones, Asberry Jones

K. Samuel Knapp, Robert Kinds

L. Eliza Landgford, John Lowry, Edward Lamb, James H. Lauraned

M. Ann Moore, Jeremiah Martin, John M'Kee, John M'Intire, Wm M'Clennen, Hugh M'Connel, Wm. M'Donald, Thomas Mountjoy, John Malott, John Murphy, Benjamin Moore, Joseph Moore, Michael Mayuugh, Jacin Miller

N. Orrice Newton

O. Recruiting Officer Archabald Orry

P. Benj. Payne, James Powers, Margaret Parker, David Peters, Sarah Peters, John Pritchott

The Mirror, Washington Kentucky   The Eagle, Maysville, Kentucky

R. Charles Rumsey 2, Cardiff T. Rawlings, Wm. B. Robertson, Elijah Redmond, Wm. Richards, Samuel Robb, Thomas Rowland, Phinebas G. Rice, James Riley
S. Rulef Smith 2, James Shelton, Wm. Steel, Thomas Steers, Wm. St. Clair, Nathan Smith & Co., Levin Stewart, John Savage, Joseph Spurrier, Samuel B. Shepard
T. Wm. P. Thomas, James Tolle 2, John Tribbey
V. Thomas Vincent, Peter Vandeventer, Frederick C. Viers
W. Joshua Whitington, Wm. Watkins, Wm. Woodhouse, Jared Woodworth, Elisha Walls, Henry Wier, Oliver Winchel 2, Francis A. Wilkey, Wm. Walker, Joseph Wallingsford, Simeon Walton, Sally Wilson, John Wilson, Henry Williams, George Williams, George White
Y. Henry Yoder,
John Roe P.M. Maysville July 1, 1818

800 yds. Tow linen and a handsomely assorted lot of bent Iuniata Barr Iron, Wholesale or retail on terms advantageous to the purchaser Also 3 large strong tight new Orleans Boats, for sale by Phillips & Stout, Maysville, KY June 8, 1818

PHILLIPS & STOUT Having succeeded James Chambers Esq. In the Storage & commission business, in Maysville, Ky. beg leave to offer to the public their services as Commission Merchants. They hope from their experience in that line of business, with the addition of large and convenient ware houses, to be able to render general satisfaction to those who may confide to them their business at this place. They are also preparing a large and convenient yard for the express purpose of storing tobacco, where the farmer and others can be accommodated with every convenience for inspection. They have on hand the following articles which they will sell low for Cash or approved paper at sixty days.24 bales of Tennessee Cotton, Loaf, Lump, Prussian and new-Orleans Sugars by the barrel. Molasses do Rock Candy by the box3,4,6,8 &10d Rolled Iron, Sickles by the dozen,8-10 window glass by the box Shot, assorted sizes do Feathers by the sack A complete assortment of Writing, Printing and Wrapping Paper. Paste boards by the gross Plated Saddle Trees assorted, of the latest fashions Flour by the single barrel or quantity Orders from our friends at a distance for any articles which this market will afford, will be attended to with punctuality and dispatch. Maysville, May 1, 1818

115 Acres First rate Land for sale. Will be sold at public venue, on Saturday the 25th of July, the above quantity of land, the property of Laban

The Mirror, Washington Kentucky   The Eagle, Maysville, Kentucky

Mitchell, lying five miles above Maysville on the Ohio river in Mason County, KY. A proportion of the purchase money will be required at the time of purchasing and a credit will be given on the balance to be made known on the day of sale. Sale to commence at ten o'clock A.M. at the home of the said Mitchell who will make a general warrantee deed for the above property. LEWIS BRIDGES for LAVAN MITCHELL......(SPELLED DIFFERENTLY)

Mason County, Kentucky Sct. TAKEN UP, by Stokes Anderson, living near Anderson's Ferry on Tucky How Ridge, a dark colored mare, about thirteen and a half hands high, right fore foot cloven, a little gray about the head from age, no brands perceivable, suppose to be about sixteen or seventeen years old, appraised to eight dollars. Given under my hand, this 1st day of July 1818 Thomas Hixson, j.p.m.c,

50$ Reward. Ran way from the subscriber in Mayslick, Kentucky on the 30 of June last, a Negro man named BEN, about 23 years of age, suppose to be about five feet eleven inches high, stout and well proportioned, of a dark complexion, no other marks recollected, is very bold, and will no doubt attempt to pass himself for a free man - He took with him a small bay horse, saddle and bridle. Had on when he went away a pair of tow linen pantaloons, cloth coat and rorum hat; having a pair of hankeen pantaloons and gingham roundabout coat with him, it is expected he will change his clothing. The above reward will be given if taken any where out of this state, and all reasonable expenses paid if brought home and twenty-five Dollars if taken in this state. THOMAS T. SUMMERS. July 2, 1818

A Valuable Tract of Land For Sale, Lying on the Ohio river in Brown County, Ohio, one and a half miles below Maysville, containing about 557 acres of nearly fell first rate bottom land. - Terms of payment are one third in hand, one third on the first day of June, 1819, the other third on the first day of June, 1820. A general warrantee, deed will be given when the last payment is made. Mr. James Powers of Maysville has a plat of said survey and will show it to any person wishing to purchase, and make known the price. N. BEASLY for JESSEE M'KEY. Maysville June 31, 1818

A BARGAIN. An elegant Wagon for sale. For terms apply to GEORGE W. DAULTON. Maysville, June 25, 1818

The Mirror, Washington Kentucky   The Eagle, Maysville, Kentucky

NEW GOODS The subscribers have just received and are now opening A Complete Assortment of Spring Goods, while they are determined to sell at a very reduced prices for CASH land HORNE & HITCHISON

KENTUCKY LEWIS CIRCUIT COURT, ser April term 1818 . Martha Johnston, Compt't against Daniel Johnston Def't.. This day came the complainant by Walker Reid. Her Counsel and pled her bill in this cause, and the Sheriff having returned the subpoena issued against the defendant, from which it appears other satisfaction of the court and from other testimony, that the said defendant is not an inhabitant of these commonwealth of having talked to   appearance herein agreeable law and the rules of this court. Therefore on motion of all complainant by her counsel, it is ordered that unless the said defendant appear here on or before the first day of the next July term of this court and answer the complainant's bid (the prayer and objects of which is to obtain a divorce from the said defendant on the grounds of abandonment for upwards of three years and his living in adultery with another woman.) That the same will be taken as confession against him and a decree entered into agreeable to the prayer thereof. And it is further ordered that a copy of this order be forwith inserted for eight weeks successively in some public newspaper of this commonwealth authorized to make such publication. A copy attest Jos. Robb. C.l.cc.

TOWN LOTS FOR SALE The subscriber has for sale, ten or twelve small building lots, lying between Second and Third streets, for which he will give a very considerable credit - Any persons wishing to purchase ..by making an early application. Stephen Lee Maysville July 7, 1818

SHINGLES FOR SALE The subscriber wishes to inform the public that he has constantly on hand best quality warranted shingles. His yard is near Mr. Amos Cotwine's landing, where the above shingles are manufactured and where those wishing to purchase can be always supplied. N. Hooker. Maysville July 17, 1818

FOURTH OF JULY. The subscribers have just received from Philadelphia and are now opening at their former stand, on the corner of Market and Second streets, a large assortment of Summer & Fall goods, and from New Orleans, a quantity of Sugar, Equal in quality to any in this market, which they will sell by the barrel or retail! Those wishing to purchase will do well to call and judge for themselves, as they are determined to sell cheap

The Mirror, Washington Kentucky The Eagle, Maysville, Kentucky

goods for Cash or such country produce as suits our market. SHUTZ, HIXSON & Co. Maysville July 9, 1818

MAYSVILLE ABOLITION SOCIETY. The members of the above names Society are requested to be particular in their attendance at the house of Amos Corwine, Jr. On Second street (near the Steam Saw-mill) on Friday the 4th of September, next, at precisely 10 O'clock A.M. All persons being desirous to become acquainted with our motives, will please to attend Amos Corwine, Jr. Sec'y. Maysville, July 1, 1818

For Sale. The subscriber has for sale, one two horse, plantation Wagon, for pleasure, or Dearbon do. And one Ox-carts and a Yoke of Oxen, which he will sell low for Cash. David Lindsay. Maysville June 24, 1818

NOTICE is hereby given. All persons having just claims against the estate of John Boyd dec'd. late of Wilson's Bottom, Lewis County, KY to exhibit their claims, legally proven for adjustment within one year from the date hereof; and all those indebted to said estate are requested to make immediate payment to JOHN BOYD executor June 2,, 1818

Maysville Thursday July 16th 1818 General Andrew Jackson has arrived in Nashville, and was joyfully received by his fellow-citizens.

Interesting St. Louis, June 19 Manuel Lisa, Esq. Arrived here a few days ago, from his trading posts on the Upper Missouri, with valuable cargoes of Furs, Peltry & c. & c., This enterprising gentleman is anxious to again extend our Indian trade to and beyond the Rocky Mountains. Previous to the late arrival, his establishments extended to the Pacific side of the mountains. But his parties were obliged to return to the Missouri, leaving behind them an immense quantity of valuable furs, in consequence of the hostility of the Black Feet Indians.

We learn that the Indians who reside on the river Platt and between the rivers Missouri, and Arkansas are (as usual) at war with one another. About two months ago, a party of the Pawnee, consisting of four hundred, met a war party of Osages in the plains, within 50 or 60 miles, of the Arkandsas. The advance guard of the Pawnees made a running fight, drawing after them the Osages into an ambuscade, formed by the main body of the Pawnees. The affair is said to have resulted in the entire defeat and destruction of the Osages; one only escaped out of 49 warriors. Our informant say 47 guns taken from the Osages. The Pawnees, are also at

The Mirror, Washington Kentucky   The Eagle, Maysville, Kentucky

war with the Spaniards of St a Fe: they lately defeated and killed seven Spaniards out of a hunting party they met within the limits of the United States territory. Among the baggage of the Spaniards they found concealed, a Spanish boy, about ten years old; him they spared, intending to offer him as a sacrifice "to the Great Star." This boy has been recently purchased from the priest by Mr. Lisa and providentially saved from the fire. This poor little victim was so impressed with his intended fate that (a few nights ago) he sprang from his bead and called for Mr. Lisa to protect him from the Pawnees, who were coming to burn him. And when convinced that he was in a place of safety, he declared that his dreadful apprehension, could not be done away, until he had performed a promise he had made when at the Pawnees Village, vix that if the Almighty would release him, he would have a solemn mass performed for his deliverance. Mr. Lisa says he will if possible have him gratified. His is to be sent to school and educated for the counting house. Some time ago this sanguinary band took a Pado woman prisoner and devoted her to the sacrifice; as she was pregnant, they waited her delivery before the offering should be made. However, as soon as she recovered from child-birth she stole a horse and escaped. Her infant child was immediately transfixed on a sharp pole as an offering to their god

HORRID MURDER!! As Mr. Lewis Bland of Columbus, was seeking his horses in the Indian lands on the Norton Road. From Delaware to Sandusky, at the crossing of the Little Scotio, on Wednesday the 24th he discovered a dead body, in the water lying face downward, less than twenty yards from the bridge, which on examination proved to be the body of Stephen Delando jr. Son of Mr. Stephen Delano of Cliaton township, in this county, as was ascertained by his papers - his head, on the right side was lacerated with a wound, which one of the spectators hand had fractured his skull and the eye on the left side was started from the socket, his throat was cut, at tho' the gash had not affected the wind pipe. His clothes were found in much the same state as when he was last seen. Mr Bland immediately proceeded to Mr. Ridenhour's the nearest house and proclaimed it. Mess. Bland, Carrell, Avery, Curtis, and Murray, neighbors; and Mr. Vanhorne, of this town, proceeded to examine the dead body and the result was as before states. Mr. Carrell stated that this same man to him a stranger, came by his house, (about three fourths of a mile from the tragical scene) on the Thursday before, and manifested the greatest fear and alarm for the Indians, who he said had accused him of stealing. A very strict examination was passed on the body by all present - Application was made for the Coroner of Delaware county, which is the nearest in the jurisdiction

The Mirror, Washington Kentucky The Eagle, Maysville, Kentucky

of the state of Ohio, but he was absent. - A Licarion was made to the stae's attory for the same county but he refused, alleging want of jurisdiction. It is worthy of remarks, that blood was side covered on the bridge and that the deceased's razor was found in the water near him. Hence it is evident that the deceased came to his death by violence; and that it was done by himself is contrary to the evidence For the cut in his throat does not appear sufficient, and the fracture of the scull was probably the cause of his death. It appears therefore rather to have been a bungling attempt to conceal the character of the real murder. - Then, as we look for the cause of the murder, but the violence of some other person, suspicion will rest where there is the greatest evidence, and that appears to me against the Indians. In the mean time, let the constituted authorities use energy to bring punishment the foul perpetrators of this horrid deed. While I sympathize with the venereal afflicted parent, and can as sincerely burn with holy indignation at the brutal assassins, it is well to caution the public not be sanguine that it was Indians. It is probably; but it is not certain - Columbus Monitor.

Married On Thursday evening, the 9th inst. By the Rev. Robert Wilson, Mr. William M. Pysiz of this place to Miss Jane Baldwin, daughter of Mr. Samuel Baldwin, Esq of this county.

NOTICE As I am making arrangements for moving from this part of the country to a place at considerable distance , all those indebted to me are requested to call and pay what they owe me. Those having claims against me are also requested to call, as I am prepared to pay all those to whom I am indebted. DEMSEY SEYBOLD July 14, 1818

WHO WANTS 20,000 DOLLARS? If any person wants $20,000 let him call and purchase a ticket in the FAYETTE HOSPITAL LOTTERY. There are several prizes of $10,000, $5000, and $1000 be idus many other prizes of $500, $100 and $50, not two blanks to a prize. This scheme offers a very brilliant prospect to purchasers, of acquiring fortunes with only the risk of $50 which is only the price of a Ticket in this brilliant scheme. Tickets may be had by applying at Thomas M. Duke's store Washington, or at the Office Samuel January, Sen'r & Co., Maysville July 16,1818

BANK OF FLEMINGSBURGH. The undersigned commissioners hereby give notice to the Stock holders of said Bank, that an election will be held at the court House in the town of Flemingsburgh, on the 17th day of August 1818, for electing a president and with Directors. Joshua Stockton,

The Mirror, Washington Kentucky   The Eagle, Maysville, Kentucky

Thomas Wallace, James Alexander, Thos. W. Fleming, William P. Roper Contr's. July 18, 1818

WHOLESALE QUEENS-WARE; GLASS AND CHINA STORE. THOMAS JONES, no 6, Prather's Row, Louisville, (KY) Shortly expects to receive per steam boat Et a. Cincinnati, and Buffalo, and Barge Sarah Jane,31 Hhds, 36 Boxes, 55 Crates   Glass, China and Queens-ware, Comprising almost every article of Liverpool, enameled and Cream colored ware in ordinary use, which will be opened and repacked to suit purchasers at a small advance only from the New Orleans prices, and probably lower than has ever been offered in the western country- N.B.T. Jones establishment is devoted exclusively to the above business and he expects to be constantly supplied with a complete assortment. Merchants are assured that their orders will at all times be executed with fidelity and upon the most favorable terms. Louisville, Jul 16, 1818

Nicholas Circuit: June Term 1818 John Sanderson, compl. Against Philip Richard Kendall & Robert Young, Deft's. The defendants not having entered their appearance herein agreeable to the act of assembly and the rules of the court, and it appearing to the satisfaction of the court that they are not inhabitants of this commonwealth. On motion of the complainant, it is ordered that they do so, on or before the first day of the next September term, and answer the complainants bill, that a copy of this order be inserted in some authorized newspaper of this state for two month successively. A copy attest. Lewis H. Arnold C.N.C.C. July 16, 1818

MAYSVILLE & LEXINGTON TURNPIKE ROAD. Books are opened at Maysville, Washington and Mayslick, for the reception of subscriptions to the stock of the company incorporated by an act of assembly passed at the last session for turnpiking the road from Maysville to Lexington. The liberality of the Charter granted by the legislature for the incorporation of this company cannot, it is believed fail to make the stock a profitable one, and the immense importance of the contemplated road to every class of citizens, and particularly to the agricultural interest of the country it is hoped, will produce a demand for the stock .TERMS OF SUBSCRIPTION. At the time of subscribing, a negotiable note for one tenth of the subscription must be executed payable a the Washington branch Bank; sixty days after the company shall be organized and not more than one tenth of the subscription can be called in any sixty days thereafter. John Sumrall, Johnson Armstrong, Maurice Langhorn , Contn'rs at Maysville Jas. A. Paxton, David Massie, Jno. Chambers, Commissioners at

The Mirror, Washington Kentucky   The Eagle, Maysville, Kentucky

Washington, James Morris, Jno Shotwell, commissions at Mayslick April 7th 1817

MONEY WANTED All those indebted to the subscriber, are earnestly requested to make payment on or before the first of July next, as he intends to set out for the eastward at that time, for the purpose of purchase of fresh supply goods. W.B. Shackleford Maysville, June 4 1818

EDWARD EASTON , BOOT AND SHOE MAKER, is desirous to return his sincerer thanks to the ladies and gentlemen of Maysville and vicinity, for the favors confirmed on him since he has been in this place and further wishes to inform his customers that he has removed from his former stand and has commenced business on Sutton Street between Mr. Chambers' Inn and the Market house, where he is determined to cut the best of leather, and as he has previously and will continue to give the best of wages thus given in the state to accommodate ladies and gentlemen who may be able to favor him with their custom may depend on having a steady attention paid them. And those favors will ever be gratefully acknowledged by their observant servant. Maysville June 11, 1818

TRULY IMPORTANT! The subscriber takes this method of informing the public in general, that he has commenced: the BURR MILL STONE MAKING, in Maysville, on second street, directly opposite to John Armstrong's new row, where he intends to keep a constant supply of the above mentioned articles manufactured in the first rate order of workmanship. From his long experience in the art of manufacturing French and Georgia Burrs, he hesitates not in saying with confidence, that from the particular care and attention which he intends to pay in selecting out small pieces, and in jointing and cementing them together with Plaister of Paris, in a complete manner, to give general satisfaction to those who may find it an interest to favor him with their custom. He will be able to furnish millstones from three feet and a half, to five feet in diameter. It is very evident that a millstone made in this way, can be furnished of a first rate burr, and of a uniform quality. CHARLES DOYLE.CERTIFICATE.- Dear sir, as it may be of use to you we take this opportunity to state, that the mill-stones you have made for us, of the Raccoon Bur, appear to be done in a masterly and workman - like manner, as far as we are judges, and that this opinion has frequently been expressed by experienced millers, and other men of judgment and knowledge, in that line - and therefore we do not hesitate to recommend your work to any man or concern, who may

The Mirror, Washington Kentucky   The Eagle, Maysville, Kentucky

wish to have a millstones well made. Very respectfully, SAM'L FINDLEY & Co. Chillicothe steam Mill, July 26th

BARTLET & COX, OF NEW ORLEANS. The term of partnership of the above firm, having expired, the affairs of the concern - will be settled by the subscriber. He continues business on his own account in New Orleans, where consignments and orders will meet with due and prompt attention. His establishment is in Poiid ass street, a healthy pleasant part of the city, and near the active business of the boats and shipping. NATH'L COX

HENRY MACHIR, Has just received from Philadelphia and Baltimore, a general assortment of spring and summer goods, which he will sell very cheap. Maysville, May 8, 1818 N.B. He confidently hopes that all those who are indebted to him by note or book account, will make immediate payment as he intends bringing his old business to a speedy close.

Grand Masonic Hall Lottery, (Now drawing at Lexington, Ken.) HIGHEST PRIZE $20,000, which together with most of the capital prizes, (such as three of $10,000, three of $5,000 & c.,) are still in the wheel. Present price of tickets $10. Each, but will soon rise. Tickets for sale at the counting room of Wm. B. Phillips, on Front Street, Maysville, KY Friends to the prosperity of the craft, and all who wish to obtain an independence without much trouble, are invited to purchase without delay.

TANNER'S OIL. A quantity of best quality. Tanners Oil, for sale at the store of John Armstrong. Maysville, March 27, 1818

BILLS OF EXCHANGE on New Orleans, Will be purchased at the Washington branch bank, Robert Taylor, Jnr. Cach'r, January 6, 1818

BURR MILL STONES, FOR SALE, the subscriber has on hand at Maysville, a quantity of the Racoon Burr Mill stones, of a superior quality, which he is determined to sell as low as any stones of the same quality have ever been sold in this country. Applications to the subscriber in Chillicothe, or the January, Withans & January in Maysville will be thankfully received and punctually attended to. All stones sold by me will be warranted good. Richard M'Dougal. April 10, 1818

SALT FOR SALE. The subscriber takes this method to inform the public that he has now on hand, and intends constantly to keep, at his house on Second street, nearly opposite Mr. Grinstead's brick house, a supply of the

The Mirror, Washington Kentucky   The Eagle, Maysville, Kentucky

best quality, KANHAWA SALT, Which he will dispose of at the Maysville prices by the quantity barrel or bushel. PETER GRANT Maysville, May 28, 1818 N.H. I wish o purchase a few thousand pounds of Bacon and a few hundred bushels of corn.

ALEXANDER R. DEPEW has fixed his residence in Maysville and will continue to practice as Counselor and Attorney at Law in the Circuit Courts of Mason, Lewis Fleming, Nicholas and Bracken. He keeps his Office on Water Street, in the first brick building below that in which Maj. John Brown resides. He will also continue to keep an office in Washington, in which Mr Athelstan Owens will attend to the reception and preparations of causes and the various branches of conveyanceing, April 17, 1818

DRUGS & MEDICINES, The subscribers have just opened adjoining the store F. SHULTZ HIXSON & Co, near the market-house a large and general assortment of DRUGS, MEDICINES, SURGEONS' INSTRUMENTS, SHOP FURNITURE, PAINTS &C &C Purchased in New York and Baltimore, and warranted to be of the first quality. We contemplate keeping on hand a sufficient quantity to supply the demands of the neighboring towns and country. Order directed to us will be thankfully received and meet with prompt attention. J & E. G. BYERS Maysville, April 24, 1818

NEW GOODS, I have just received from New York and Philadelphia, a general assortment of merchandise, which I offer at the most moderate prices: The public will do well to call where they can be well supplied. JAMES MORRISON. Maysville, May 1, 1818N.B. I expect to start to the Eastward on the first of June - all those who have been indebted to me longer than the last six months, are solicited to call and settle their accounts immediately

Important to Tanners and Distillers. J OLDS' patent Bark Mills, The subscriber being assignee of J. Olds patent Bark Mills for the states of Ohio, Kentucky and Tennessee, takes this method of informing the Tanners and Distillers in this and the adjoining states aforesaid, that they can be supplied with the above Mills by application to the subscribers in Maysville, Kentucky, or in case of his absence, apply to Messrs. January and Witham, where they will constantly be kept for sale and where any information can be had respecting the quality of them (as there are a number in operation in this place) Mr. Old's Mill being the latest improvement that has been made, are allowed by all those who have use of

The Mirror, Washington Kentucky   The Eagle, Maysville, Kentucky

them to be the best of any in the United States, for the facility of grinding and quality of bark when ground, Those Mills are also found to be equally beneficial to Distillers for grinding corn in the ear and preparing it for the stones. It has been thoroughly ascertained, that corn ground in this way (including the cobs) will produce at least one fifth more spirits than in the ordinary way. They can be put in operation improved plan of Mr. Olds' which is simple in its construction, and of course less liable to get out of repair; the cost of erecting will not exceed fifteen Dollars - the cost of the Mill with printed directions for putting them in operation will not exceed eighty Dollars. If they do not answer the purposes aforesaid, they may be returned and the money shall be refunded. The subscriber is determined to give satisfaction to all who may favor him with their custom.   A. BATES MAYSVILLE APRIL 27, 1818

ENTERTAINMENT. Sign of the Green Tree. The subscriber has opened a house of entertainment in the white house at Ellis' Ferry, on the Ohio River immediately opposite Maysville, KY where he has made repairs & arrangements to enable him to give comfortable entertainment to such travelers as may favor him with their custom. His house is pleasantly situated, on the bank of the Ohio river, and is convenient, airy and well furnished with new beds. His supply of liquors is of the best quality, and his table shall not suffer for want of variety. His stable is good and well attended to, and stores with excellent provender. He therefore hopes, from his unremitting attention, and his determination to please as far as practicable, to receive a portion of public favor.   ELIAS TAPP   June 4, 1818

TALBOTT'S HOTEL. In Millersburg, KY formerly the sign of the Red Lion. The Subscriber continues to keep Entertainment for Travellers, in the Stone home at the above sign, where he intends to do every thing in his power to please them. DANIEL TALBOTT   June 1817

To Merchants. For sale The subscribers have on hand, and intend keeping constant supplies of the following articles, which they will sell wholesale on good terms (to wit.)   White Glass Ware, well assorted, from the Charleston works, Casting well assorted, from Brush Creek Furnace, Patent Corn Shellers and Grinders. Cut Nails assorted by the keg at the Pittsburgh prices with the addition of carriage. German Glass Tumberls. Buffalo Robes by the Pack. Lintseed Oil, by the Barrel, Coperass, by the obl. Or keg of excellent quality, Paper of all descriptions, Whiskey by the bbl. Madeira & Teneriffe Wines, by the ½ pipe, bbl or half bbl.   Sundry other

The Mirror, Washington Kentucky   The Eagle, Maysville, Kentucky

articles too numerous to be inserted - the whole of which will be sold low for Cash, or on liberal credits to good men. Samuel January, Sen. & Co. April 24.

MILLSTONES (Of a superior quality) will in future be made at the Red River Quarry, and sold by SPENCER ADAMS & JAMES DANIEL. If any of our Mill Stones should not prove good, we bind ourselves to furnish more at the quarry until they do prove good. The prices of Stones at the quarry are as follows, to wit - For five feet stones $200 per pair; for four feet $150, for three feet 80; All other sizes in the same proportion as above. The price of a runner will be two thirds the price of a pair. All persons wishing to purchase will apply to the undersigned in Winchester, KY or to William B. Shackleford, in Maysville, either personally or by letter, which will be thankfully received and punctually attended to JAS DANIEL March 27, 1818

New Store, and all new goods. David Morrison. Has just received from Philadelphia and New York, and is now opening in the new brick building situated between Mr. J. Morrison and J. K. Sumrall's Stores, a general and well selected assortment of Spring & Summer Goods, consisting of Dry Goods Queen's Ware, Hard Ware, Groceries &c. &c. Which were purchased under the most favorable circumstances, and principally for cash, which enables him to offer them as low as any goods of the same quality can be purchased in this place. Maysville, April 17th 1818 N.B. I wish to purchases a few thousand lbs of good Bacon for which I will give nine cents per pound, on half in cash and the other in merchandise. D.M.

KANHAWA SALT. Langhorne & Payne, have constantly on hand a large quantity of the above article, which they offer for sale by the barrel or single bushel. February 27, 1818

TRULY IMPORTANT TO DISTILLERS. The undersigned lately from Philadelphia, wishes to inform the citizens of Kentucky and Ohio that he now carries on the Copper Smiths business, in Maysville Kentucky, where he is completely prepared to furnish stills and all kinds of copper work, of superior quality and workmanship to any heretofore known in these parts, with large caps and worms, at one dollar per gallon, for the capacity of the still body; and other work in proportion - It may be necessary to mention that he has introduced a new plan of distilling with goose-neck and heaters, whereby the still can be run with safety, one third faster than on the old plan. He has also for sale Sheet copper assorted, Plitters, Sodder, Borax,

The Mirror, Washington Kentucky   The Eagle, Maysville, Kentucky

Block tin and Still cocks, which he will sell on the most moderate terms for cash. DANIEL GRAUL Maysville march 27th 1817. N.B. orders directed to Mr. Jno. Armstrong, merchant at my shop in 2d below market street, will be thankfully received and punctually attended to. D. G.

FOR SALE, AT D & S. LEE'S GROCERY STORE. On Front-street. Maysville, a complete list of the chartered banks in the U. States. Price 12 ½ cents. EPHRAIM BRICK Maysville Dec 5, 1817

FOR SALE, A complete set of nailing tools for making cut nails, with two headers and three cutters. JOHN BROWN Maysville, May 14, 1818

DISSOLUTION. The copartnership heretofore existing under the firm of Morrison & Mackey, is this day dissolved by mutual consent, All those indebted to said firm, are requested to make payment to William Mackey, either by cash or their notes. Those having claims will also present them as above for payment. JAMES MORRISON WILLIAM MACKEY May 3rd 1818

NOTICE. The subscriber has just received from Philadelphia and Baltimore, an extensive assortment of Spring & summer goods, which he will sell low for cash. ALSO-A general assortment of BOLTING CLOTHS best quality. JOHN ARMSTRONG. Maysville, May 21, 1818 N.B. I have a large assortment of Juniatta Bar Iron on hand and for sale. J.A.

NEW GOODS. We have just received from Philadelphia and are now opening at our old Store on the corner of Front and Main Cross Streets, a very general assortment of MERCHANDISE, Well adapted to the present and approaching seasons, which we can sell as low as any in the place. We request our friends to call and examine for themselves. LANDGHORNE & PAYNE. Maysville, June 18, 1818

ALL NEW GOODS. The subscribers wish to inform their friends and the public in general, that they have just received from Philadelphia, and are now opening at their store room on Water Street, next door above Messrs. Langhorne & Hutchinsons's store very general assortment of Merchandise, Suited for the present and approaching seasons, all of which they are determined to sell at the most reduced prices for cash or approved country produce. WILLIAM TUREMAN & SON. Maysville June 11, 1818

The Mirror, Washington Kentucky   The Eagle, Maysville, Kentucky

CASH AGAIN. ALL those indebted to the subscribers will avoid trouble and confer an obligation on us by closing their accounts immediately MARTIN & JANUARY Maysville, 8h June 1818

PUBLIC NOTICE is hereby given, That in pursuance of the act of assembly, passed the 31st day of January, 1818 entitled "An act to establish a Turnpike road, leading from the mouth of Big Sandy, through the counties of Greenup and Lewis, in a direction to Flemingsburgh" the undersigned commissioners appointed by the said act, to le the opening and keeping in repair of the said road, will meet at the Court House in the county of Greenup, on the fourth Monday in July next; and proceed to let the same, to the person or persons who will open the said road, agreeable to the provisions of the said act, and constantly keep the same in good repair for the shortest period of time not to exceed twenty years. Bond and approved security from the undertaker or undertakers, in the penal sum of ten thousand dollars payable to the commonwealth, conditioned for the faithful discharge of the duties required by the said act, will be required. It is required that the road shall be completed in one year from the time the same is undertaken. The sum of $1000, allowed by the said act, to be raised by subscription, is already raised and greater encouragement is expected.   ARRON STRATTON, THO BRAGG, OB'D. S. TIMBERLAKE, GEORGE POAGE, JOHN HOCKADAY. June 11, 1818

WILLIAM M. POYNTZ, has just received from New-Orleans, and offers for sale at his Ware house, Corner of Third and Main Cross streets, Maysville, the following articles: SUGAR, COFFEE, MOLASSES, TRAIN OIL in barrels, SALMON in ? Kegs And a variety of other articles in the Grocery line, all of which will be sold reasonable terms for CASH. May 1, 1818

WASHINGTON INN D. MASSIE Has removed from his former stand, (traveler's Inn) to a large and convenient Brick House, at the corner of Water and Market Streets - He solicits the patronage of his friends, and of traveling gentlemen and ladies generally. Maysville, KY June 23, 1818

Maysville, Kentucky Thursday, September 17, 1818

DOMESTIC GOODS.   Corner of Market and Water streets.   The subscriber has just received a consignment of domestic goods, which will be sold usually low by the piece- Merchants and others wishing to purchase in part way …By calling and examining these goods before the purchase.

The Mirror, Washington Kentucky   The Eagle, Maysville, Kentucky

Also, 4000 Dozens Cotton Yarn, 6000 lbs Lead and Shot. Oaleans Sugar, by the barrel or otherwise, Buffalo Robes dressed in the best manner, Bridgeport Glass, 8 by 10 & 10 by 12, by the box. Hollow Glass assorted in boxes, Writing, Letter, Wrapping, Tea and Printing Paper, by the ream. The Rusow Glass and Paper will be sold at the manufacturers prices without freight. Johnston Armstrong Maysville August 12, 1818 N.B. All those indebted are requested to call and settle their respective accounts.

Entertainment. The subscriber has opened a House of Entertainment in the WHITE HOUSE. At the North end of Mayslick, Kentucky, where he is prepared to entertain each traveler, as way favor him with their custom. His house is pleasantly situated and convenient. His stables is good, well attended to and stoped (sic) with excellent provender, and from his unremitting attention and determination to please as far as is in his power, he hopes to receive a portion of public patronage. C. V. Anderson August 13, 1818

Taken up by Matthew Burris, living on the waters of Cabin Creek, a black Mare supposed to be about 20 years old, 14 ½ hands high, 3 shoes on branded on the near shoulder, but not legible and very weak eyes, appraised for five dollars by Thomas Bogges and Bailey Bryma before me, this 27th day of June 1818 Thomas Parker? L.C. A copy teste, Jos. Roms? C.L.D.C.

To Rent. The subscriber will rent the farm on which he now lives, opposite Maysville. There is about thirty acres under fence, sixteen of which it is meadow, with a large orchard. The dwelling house is spacious and convenient and the situation is a good one for a tavern. A. Mitchell. Sept. 1, 1818

Notice. The subscriber wishes to inform the citizens of Maysville and its vicinity in general, that he has commenced the shoe and boot making business in all its various branches on Second Street, a few doors above the printing office, on the opposite side of the street. He flatters himself that he can furnish good work, and of the newest fashions as he intends keeping the best of material also the best of workmen. Levin Stewart. Maysville, July 21 1818.

Coping with Dover. The subscriber hereby takes the liberty of giving general notice, that the proprietor of the town of Dover, recently laid off on the Ohio river, Mason County, Ky. Have according to their abilities and judgments taken the privilege of changing the names of the town of

The Mirror, Washington Kentucky   The Eagle, Maysville, Kentucky

Levana, and calling it Calais, which will appear to the public in printed advertisement for a sale of lots. I therefore wish it to be known to the public that this name (Calais) is absolutely a fictitious one and in this case made us of (on my opinion) contrary to law. I have under a privilege in law, laid off the town of Levana myself, & without infringing upon the name of any neighboring town, or using ridiculous means have called its name Levana and according to law had it on record, and paid the clerk's fees, and I flatter myself that when the proprietors of the town of Dover do so, that no man or set of men of rational sense will ever endeavor to convert the name of Dover into Calais, without first showing good cause for the same, and then have it done according to law. When I advertised the first sale of lots in Levana, I gave it great praise, which certainly Dover is worthy of for it s many natural advantages, but I never once described the disadvantages of any neighboring town, because I supposed no gentleman should do so. It likewise had knowledge enough to know that it would be injurious to my interest. The public are therefore informed that this place Levana will be known by its original name until changed by better authority than the authors of the Dover Advertisement. I remain the public's Humble servant. William Butt. Levana August 23, 1818

$5 Reward. Strayed or stolen from the pasture of John Chamberlain, in Mason county Ky. 0on the road leading from Washington to Charleston. Bay Mare, about 15 hands high 4 years old, past a small star in her forehead, right hind foot white to the first joint above the hoof. The above reward will be given to any person who will bring back the said mare, and deliver her to the subscriber at John Chamberlain's above mentioned. James Stephens. September 1, 1818

For sale, a House and lot. Handsomely situated, adjoining the town of Maysville, for terms apply to Ennis Duncan, Jun'r. Maysville, August 16, 818

For Sale, the subscriber offers for sale 200 acres First rate land, living in Brown county Ohio, 20 miles from Maysville, on the waters of Eagle creek in Ronaeils's ? settlement, on the Sugartree Ridge, and within about five miles of the county seat. There are two excellent cabins and about four acres of cleared and under fence. For terms, apply to the Printer or Nathaniel Beasley in Decatur or Wm. Laycock near the premises. James Stone. September 8, 1818

The Mirror, Washington Kentucky   The Eagle, Maysville, Kentucky

Notice. Mr. John M'Nutt, Please notice that I will attend at the house of Mr. David Maxsie, in the town of Maysville, Mason County, Kentucky, on Saturday, the six day of October next, to take the deposition of Samuel Strong, to be read in evidence in a certain suit now depending in the Mason circuit court, wherein you are the complainant and I am defendant. You will attend between the hours of 12 and 3 o'clock. Your most obedient. John Holdeman. Setp. 9, 1818

Thursday September 17, 1818

Counterfeiting. This business continues to flourish beyond all former example. About a dozens persons were arrested near Cincinnati last week. They had counterfeited the notes of the united Stakes Bank, the bank of New York, the Bank of Pennsylvania, the Bank of Delaware, the Bank of Tennessee, the Bank of Kentucky, three of the Cincinnati banks, and the banks of Dayton and Warren, in this state. The following persons are among the number confined at Cincinnati : Samuel Reddington, Ethan Olney, James Bannon, James B. Hawkins, Davis B. Talbot, Stanfield Moore and Bela Avery.

On the evening of the 22nd ult. An Indian of the Wyandott tribe was murdered by some of his relatives, near the mouth of the river Huron of Lake Erie. The circumstances in brief are as follows- and tend to show the continuance of that superstition, which characterizes the Indians, notwithstanding their intercourse with the whites. It appears that two Wyandotts, residing at Maklen, and relatives of the deceased, had been informed by Captain Jonny, an Indian living at the Huron river, and also a relative that a Shawnee Indian had come to his death by the witchcraft of an old Indian woman and her son Mike, and that in order to avert the vengeance of the Shawnee it would be necessary to kill them and furthermore, that the death of Walk on the Water, who died last June, was caused by the same old woman's witchcraft, it was determined to kill the old woman and her son - and for that purpose they crossed over on the 22nd ult and succeeded in the course of the evening in killing the latter at his cabin. The old woman was not at home. The next day while endeavoring to persuade her to accompany them into the woods, as they said to drink whisky, there were discovered by Dr. Wm. Brown and Mr. Oliver Williams, who had received that morning insinuations of their intentions and owing to the exertions of these gentlemen, the woman's life was preserved and one of the Indians taken, who is now confined in the jail in this city - the others escaped by swiftness of foot. On the examination of

The Mirror, Washington Kentucky   The Eagle, Maysville, Kentucky

the Indian taken it appeared that the old woman shortly after the death of the Shawnee, had entered his cabin, and in a voice of exultation, called upon him, saying "Shawnee man I where are You that mock me? - You thought that you would live forever - You are gone and I am here - Come _ Why do you not come? _ She is said to have made use of nearly the same words in the cabin of Walks on the Water, shortly after his death. Detroit Gazette.

Indian Customs.   Bull Head - This celebrated warrior, chief of the Seminoles, in the lower part of East Florida, died about the month of June last. Four of his handsome horses and his favorite Negro were buried on the occasion.

A robber Caught. Norfolk, August 14. The French schr. Les Florentine arrived here on the 21st ult from Martinique and brought 2000 dollars in specie. As it was after sun down when she anchored in our harbor, it was thought best to let the specie remain on board for the night. Next morning however, it was found that the whole of the money had vanished, and that the mate whose name was John Garonde, had also become invisible. It was not doubted that the said Garonde and the specie had made their exit simultaneously and it was strongly suspected that two Frenchmen of this town who reside in Little Water Street (both cronies of his) were accomplices in the robbery. The evidence against him, however, was not satisfactory enough to commit them upon, and Garonde was supposed to have made off with the booty. But on Tuesday night last, about 10 o'clock, he and three other Frenchmen (including the two before alluded to) were accidentally seen to enter the house of one Joseph, a petty shop keeper in Portsmouth, by a gentleman of that town who presently collected a large party of citizens and conducted them to the spot. They surrounded the house and appeared two of them, but Garonde, the principal rogue, and another named Antoine, were missing. A strict search was made for them, but without success. In a hack room lay an ill looking fellow on a mattress which was spread on the floor. He was made to rise and while on of the magistrates who came with the guard was examining him, one of the party carelessly rolled over the mattress with his foot when to the surprise of all present there appeared a small trap door in the floor. Just large enough to admit a man through it. One of the citizens immediately descended it into a cellar, nearly half full of water, and with the help of a candle presently found the culprit Garonde, who with the other two were then sent to jail. Antoine, it was conjectured had fled over to Norfolk, where he resides. Upwards of $600 of gold and silver were found upon Garonde, quilted in

The Mirror, Washington Kentucky   The Eagle, Maysville, Kentucky

kind of a ? and wrapped round his body. He had a horse and chair at the door and who that might have set off for Petersburg, having left 100 with the person from whom he hired by way of a pledge for their return. About 600 more were found the next day in possession of Antoine, and he was sent to keep his worthy friends comrades in jail in Portsmouth. The whole sum recovered is between 12 and $1400

Caution   Under this head, a Providence paper states that on the 6th inst. Two persons were apprehended in that town & examined before Judge Marlin, on suspicion of passing bills of fictitious bank. They had in their possession about $4,900 in new and aud handsome bills, purporting to be of the Bank of Sandusky Bay, Blommingville, State of Ohio. The bills , a number of which they passed, are signed by A. Young, Cashier, and A. Ransom, President. The judge discharged them, although it is believed that there is no such bank.

Grand Lodge of Kentucky. At a grand annual communication of the M.W. the Grand Lodge of Kentucky, begun and held at Mason's Hall in Lexington on the last Monday, being the 31st day of August, A. I. 5818. A.D. 1818, the following brethren were elected officers for the ensuing twelve months, viz. Them. W. Thomas Bodley, C.M. N.W. Jas. W. Denny, D.C.M. W.D.G. Cowan, S.C.W. W. S. H. Woodson, F.G. W. Rev. C.W. Cloud, G. Ch. Thos. T. Bahr, G.S.C. Gabriel Tandy, G. Treas. Henry Clay, G. orator, Geo. B. Knight, G. Mer., J. M'Kinney, Jun. C.S.D. Philip Feizer, G. H. Dea. N. S. Porter , G. inr. Fran. Walker, C.S. & t.

Obituary. Died at his residence on the Glesuat Ridge, on the 31st ultimo, the venerable General Arthur St. Clair, in the eighty fourth year of his age. (two column obituary)

Married on Thursday, the 10th inst. By the Rev. Jesse Holton, Mr. Abijam Casto, of Maysville, to Miss Susan Ballenger, of Bracken county.

Notice. The Capital Stock of the Newport Bank having been taken, and one fifth thereof paid in, notice is hereby given that an election for a President and eight Directors for said Bank, will be held at the Court-House, in the town of Newport, on Wednesday the 7t^h day of October next. James Taylor, John M'Kinney, Thos. D. Carneal, John B. Lindsey, Wm. Caldwell, Commr's. Newport Ky, Sept 1st 1818.

The Mirror, Washington Kentucky   The Eagle, Maysville, Kentucky

Notice. Messrs. Bazil Dalce, John Coburn, Peter A.G. Stewart, Robert Moor, Rees Thomas, Henry Thomas, Silas Thomas, John Beggs, and Hannah his wife, Daniel Malatt and Catherine his wife, William Wright and Elizabeth his wife, heirs at law of John Thomas Deceased. Take Notice, that on the 29th and 30th days of next month, at the house of Nathaniel Beasley in St. Clairsville, in the County of Adams, and State of Ohio, I will take sundry depositions to be read in evidence, in the suit in chancery depending in the Mason Circuit Court, wherein I am complainant and you are defendants. You will please attend. Your most obedient, John Rains. September 15, 1818.

Mr. Daniel Johnston, Take Notice, that on the Friday and Saturday before the third Monday in October next, at the house of Hugh Hannah, Esq. In Lewis County, I shall take the deposition of Jane Miller, William Hannah, and others - And on the third Monday of said month, at the court house of Lewis County, I shall take the deposition of Hugh Hannah, as evidence, in the suit in chancery brought by me against you in the Lewis Circuit Court for a divorce. Martha Johnston. September 15, 1818

Who wants 20,000 Dollars? If any person wants $20,000 let him call and purchase a Ticket in the Fayette Hospital Lottery. There are several prizes of $10,000, $5,000 and $1,000, besides many other prizes of $500, $100 and $50 not two blanks to a prize. This scheme offers a very brilliant prospect to purchasers of acquiring fortunes with only the risk of $10, which is only the price of a ticket in this brilliant scheme. Tickets may be had by applying at Thomas M. Duke's Store, Washington, or at the office Samuel January Sen'r & Co. Maysville. July 16, 1818

Town Lots for sale, in Maysville, Ky. The subscriber wishes to dispose of a number of building lots of ground, situated near the center of town, lying on Water and either side of Fish Street. The latter street having been graduated from second street to the river, which must render it one of the most important landings of the place. License is granted by the county court for establishing a Ferry at this landing and the local situation warrants the conclusion that the ? cannot be distant. Where this will be the grand crossing. The attention of ? of enterprise is solicited under a full belief that the principal will justify the experiment. The sale of lots shall accommodate the purchases if possible the terms are inclusive. Joseph K. Ficklin, Maysville August 3rd 1818.

The Mirror, Washington Kentucky   The Eagle, Maysville, Kentucky

Wanted. One or two boys from 14 to 18 years old to apprentice to learn the art of Printing. Boys of good character and in obviously inclined who can read and write may meet with advantageous terms. Immediate applications at the Eagle Office.

Bartlet & Cox, of New Orleans. The term of partnership of the above firm, having expired, the affairs of the concern will be settled by the subscriber. He continues business on his own account, in New Orleans, where consignments and orders will meet with the most prompt attention. His establishment is in Poind ass street a healthy pleasant part of the city and near the active business of the boats and shipping. Nath'l Cox. Nov. 3, 1817

One Dollar. Will be given in current bank notes, for merchantable Wheat delivered in the Maysville Steam Mill on a credit of sixty days. Those indebted to the above establishment are requested to make immediate payment. In future there will be no credit given in the war of retail. Thomas Hixson. August 12, 1818

A Caution. To all persons not to take an assignment on a note for $25, given by me in Feb 1816 to Samuel Davis, late of this county. Having once paid the amount to him, I am determined not to pay it a second time unless legally compelled herein. Charles Pelham. Mason County, Set 2, 1818

Mill Stones (of superior quality) Will in the future be made at the Red River Quarry and sold by Spencer Adams and James Daniel. If any of our mill stones should not prove good, we bind ourselves to furnish more at the quarry until they prove good. The prices of stones at the quarry are as follows, to wit. For five feet stones $200 per pair, for four feet $150, for three feet $ al together sizes in the same proportion. The price of a runner will be two times the price of a pair. All persons wishing to purchase will apply to the undersigned in Winchester, Ky or to William B. Shackleford in Maysville, either personally or by letter, which will be thankfully received and punctually attended to Jas. Daniel. March 27, 1818

A valuable tract of land for sale. Lying on the Ohio river in Brown county, Ohio once and a half miles below Maysville, containing about 537 Acres nearly all first rate bottom land - Terms of payment are one third in hand, one third on the first day of June, 1819, and the other third on the first day of June, 1820. A general warrantee deed will be given when the last payment is made. Mr. James Powers of Maysville has a plat of said survey

The Mirror, Washington Kentucky   The Eagle, Maysville, Kentucky

and will shew it to any person wishing to purchase and make known the price. N. Beasley for Jesse M'Key. Maysville June 31, 1818

Positively the last Notice. In my absence to the eastward, Capt. ? (Stephen?) Lee will attend to the collection & settlement of all accounts due to me. Therefore, all those indebted in any way to the late firms of Sumrall & Co. Jno & John Sumrall or the subscriber will please call at my counting room, and make payment ot Capt. Lee by the first day of Septemeber next, as all unsettled accounts at that time, will be placed in the hands of the proper officers for collection. Jos. K. Sumrall. Maysville, July 25th 1818.

A friendly call. We wish to set out for a supply of goods on the 16th of next month. Those indebted to us will please make payment on or before that time. It is to be hoped that more attention will be paid to this, than former notices of the same kind, as we shall be under the painful necessary of putting into the hands of the proper officers for collection, all debts which will be due at the aforesaid time, without discrimination of persons. Langhorne & Hutchinson. August 13, 1818

Take Notice. As I intend on moving to the Missouri in the spring, I wish to sell a valuable tract of land. Containing two hundred acres, sixty of which is in high cultivation. Situated on the bank of the Ohio River, three miles above Maysville, in the state of Ohio, with and established ferry on the same. A general warrantee deed will be given. Any person wishing to purchase can apply to the subscriber living on the premises. John Ellis. August 15, 1818

The Eagle, Maysville Kentucky, March 16, 1825

Communications. Mr. Collins: As many of your readers are not acquainted with the proceedings of the court of appeals, and as there was a dolful piece in your last, signed a Native Kentuckian, you will oblige several of your subscribers by publishing the following brief account of them. Court of Appeals. On Thursday the 3d of February, the court met in the senate chamber in Frankfort, present, Chief Justice Barry, and Associate Justices Haggin and Trimble. , O. G. Waggoner administrated to them the oaths of office. They then took their seats, and Col. R. Taylor, Sergeant of the Court, proclaimed the court of appeals for the commonwealth of Kentucky opened. Francis P. Blair was appointed clerk and B. Hickman tipstaff and crier." The court then heard several motions,

The Mirror, Washington Kentucky   The Eagle, Maysville, Kentucky

and in the course of proceedings "the attorney general, Solomon P. Sharp, moved the court, on behalf of the commonwealth, in enter as order and cause it to be served upon Achilles Sneed, Esq. Requiring him to deliver over to the clerk of the court, al the papers, records, property, & c., belonging to the clerk's office of the late court of appeals, and it was entered accordingly. Mr. Sharp inquired whether it would not be necessary for lawyers, intending to practice in the court, to take the oaths prescribed by law; the court took time to consider, and the next day decided that it would.   Whereupon John J. Crittenden, S. P. Sharp, Jacob Swigert, Thomas Triplett, Thos. B. Monroe, John S. Chapman, George M. Beall, Charles S. Bibb, John Pyane, Preston S. Lowburrow and Lewis Sanders, Esqrs. Came forward and were qualified as attorneys of the court." The court then proceeded to business. "The clerk having communicated to Mr. Sneed, (in a very friendly letter) the order of the court requiring him to deliver over the papers, &c. above mentioned, and Mr. Sneed refusing, the sergeant was directed to serve the said order officially. This duty being performed, and Mr. Sneed having failed to comply therewith, the attorney general, on behalf of the commonwealth, moved the court to issue a summons, requiring Mr. Sneed to appear and shew cause why he should no be attached for contempt of the court, which was ordered accordingly." Shortly afterwards, "Mr. Sneed appeared in court in pursuance of the summons served on him, and Mr. Crittenden, as his attorney, moved the court for time until tomorrow morning to make up and submit his defense for the alleged contempt of the court, in not delivering the papers, records, &c., "The attorney general suggested, that so far as respected Mr. Sneed's defense, there could be no objection to granting time, provided he submitted to the authority of the court, and delivered up the public papers, records, &c in his possession."   "Mr. Crittenden urged the propriety of giving time." "The court intimated a disposition to give the solicited time, provided a pledge were given that Mr. Sneed would then deliver the papers, &c. Mr. Crittenden observed that he was not authorized to give such a pledge. "The court then gave time until tomorrow morning for Mr. Sneed to make his defense for the alleged contempt; and on motion of the attorney general, issued an order directing the tipstaff and crier to accompany the clerk of the court, with such assistance as might be necessary, and deliver over to him the papers, records, &c. belonging to the court, now in the office of the late clerk. "Saturday, Feb. 5 - It having been reported to the court that he papers, records &c. so far as in the possession of Mr. Sneed, had been delivered in to the possession of the clerk, on motion of the attorney general, the proceedings against Mr. Sneed for contempt were ordered to be discontinued."   After the court had proceeded to business some time, "it was represented to the court, that he whole of the books, papers, &c. had not been obtained form the office of the former clerk,, but that the most important portion of them had been withdrawn, previous to the entry of the officers for the court, on motion of the attorney general, it was ordered that an attachment issue against Mr. Sneed for withholding said books, and papers, returnable on Monday morning "Monday, Feb. 7." The court again commenced its session "It appearing that the order of the court directing the sergeant and tipstaff to deliver over the books and records of the clerk's office of the former court, had not been fully executed, they were ordered to proceed and complete the execution of the said order. "Mr. Sneed appeared in court, to answer the argument against him for contempt, and having answered inquiries put to him by the attorney general, the court proceeded to fine him ten pounds." (And here I would remark, that some of the questions put to Mr. Sneed by the attorney general, Mr. Sharp, might have been improper, as we frequently see even the best lawyers sometimes ask improper questions.) "The court then adjourned to the last Wednesday in March next." To me both the court and attorney general seem to have acted with firmness and propriety. Bracken county meeting. At a respectable meeting held in the town of Augusta and County of Bracken, on Tuesday, Feb 22, 1825, for the purpose of taking into consideration the constitutionality of the course pursued by our last legislature, in the removal of the judges of the court of appeals- when the Hon. Harbin Moore was nominated and unanimously chosen president, Capt. Wil. Buckner (sic) and Col. Hawkins as vice presidents, and F.A.W.H. Davis secretary. Resolved, that this meeting adjourn to meet at this place, Saturday, 9 O'clock, March 5th. Saturday morning, March 5th - a small number of citizens of this county met at the Presbyterian meeting house pursuant to adjournment. President and vice presidents as above, and A.D. Keith appointed secretary in place of F.A.W.H. Davis, resigned. Resolved, that the speakers be limited to an hour in opening, and a half hour in closing the discussion. The preamble and resolutions accompanying this, were read, and the vote being taken upon the adoption of the preamble, yeas 42, nays 22- the first resolution adopted, yeas 46, nays 21-second resolution yeas 45, nays 20-third, yeas 53, nays 14- fourth, yeas52, nays 12. H. Moor,(sic) Ch'n. Mr. A.D. Keith, Sec'y published column on the court proceedings.

We the citizens of Bracken county, convened for the purpose of taking into consideration the proceedings of the last legislature of the state of Kentucky, in reorganizing the court of appeals, and removing the judges thereof from office, in the exercise of our privileges as citizens of this state

The Mirror, Washington Kentucky The Eagle, Maysville, Kentucky

and as guardians of those free and happy institutions procured and transmitted to us by our ancestors, would betray an unpardonable degree of apathy were we to stand silent witnesses of and act, which we deem as palpable violation of the fundamental principles of our government. And while we felicitate ourselves in the excellence of our government and in the distribution of its powers admire it as a model of wisdom, we believe that the harmony of its comment parts is closely and inseparable despondent on the regular discharges of the duties of each department by the constitutional functionary. And as the constitution has provided three distinct and coordinate departments in the government, independent of each other in the exercise of their respective powers, it results that any attempt at supremacy by one department of the government over another, in opposition to the provisions of the constitution, is incompatible with the principles of liberty, by endangering tis perpetuity, and destructive of the people's happiness by producing animosity and strife in the administration of the government : Wherefore, Resolved, that it is the opinion of this meeting that the act of the last legislature, for th purpose of reorganizing the court of appeals, was an unconstitutional assumption of power on the part of the legislature. Resolved, that it is the opinion of this meeting that the judges of the court of appeals could not constitutionally be removed from office, except by impeachment or address. Resolved, that this meeting disapprove of the increase of the salary of the judges of the court of appeals and that this time of pecuniary embarrassment calls for retrenchment of the expenses of the government, instead of adding several thousand dollars to the public expenditures. Resolved, that the foregoing preamble and resolutions be signed by the chairman and secretary and published in the Maysville Eagle. Resolved that it is the opinion of this meeting that it is highly inexpedient at this time to increase the taxes, and therefore we protest against the said act of the last legislators as oppressive at this time of public embarrassment and difficulty, as a measure calculated to fill the pockets for a few individuals in office, to the impoverishment of the citizens of this common wealth at large.

To the politeness of Captain M. Langhorne, we are indebted for the National Intelligencer Extra of the 4th instant containing the following. Washington, March 4. This day, at the appointed hour, John Quincy Adams took the oath of office as President of the United States, at the capitol, and on the occasion, delivered the following inaugural address.

Maysville Meeting. A public meeting will be held in the town of Maysville on Saturday, the 26th instant, with the view of eliciting the sentiments of the

The Mirror, Washington Kentucky   The Eagle, Maysville, Kentucky

people on the constitutionality of the law of the last legislature, purporting to repeal the judges of the court of appeals out of office. The meeting will be held in the Presbyterian meeting house, and commence at 10'00 a.m. The citizens of the county are respectfully invited to attend.

Voice of the People A very large meeting was held in Estill County, on the 21st of February, when resolutions were adopted, strongly disapproving the late act of majority of the legislature, for breaking the judges or the court of appeals, and most solemnly protesting against an increase of taxation, with the view of supporting the judges of the legislative court.

PUBLIC MEETING. We are requesting to inform the citizens of the county that the people in the lower end of the Mayslick precinct design holding a public meeting at Shannon meeting house, on Saturday, the 2d of April, for the purpose of expressing their opinions on the important question, whether the old court was and is the only legitimate court, or whether the new court is now the only court of the constitution and the people. A general attendance of all on both sides of the question is requested. Public discussion is solicited; but as the object of the various meetings in the county, is to ascertain the strength of the respective parties, it is not expected that nay will claim a vote who have previously voted on the question. An after meeting is anticipated in the upper end of the precinct, probably at D. Harrison's. Voters

Gen. Jackson and Kentucky Relief Laws. The following correspondence appeared in the last Argus, and will explain itself. House of Representatives, Feb. 24, 1825. Sir- In a late number of the Argus of Western America, you are represented to have said at Lexington, on your way to this city, in November last, upon the authority of Mr. William T. Willis that "forty thousand muskets would be required to rectify the politics of Kentucky."- The undersigned having supported your election in the House of Representatives, and believing you incapable of making the remark imputed to you, deem it their duty to afford you an opportunity of contradicting the report, if untrue, for the satisfaction of all, who at any stage of the presidential contest, took an interest in your success. With sentiments of respect, we are your most obedient servants. Robt.. P. Henry, T.P. Moore, J.T. Johnson, C.A. Wickliffee.

Gen: Andrew Jackson, Senate Chamber. Washington City, Feb 22, 1825. Gentlemen -Your letter of today is received and has been read with something of surprise. I did not use the expression which you quote, "that

The Mirror, Washington Kentucky   The Eagle, Maysville, Kentucky

forty thousand muskets would be required to rectify the politics of Kentucky," nor any expression like it. My stay at Lexington was a short one, and during the time, I have no recollection of speaking at all about the local affairs of your state. It is a subject about which I should not feel myself at liberty to interfere. As to Mr. Wm. T. Willis, I have no recollection of him, nor do I believe I ever had an acquaintance with him. It is scarcely possible, that sharing as I did the politeness and hospitality of the citizens of Lexington, I should venture to insult them, by an unkind a remark. I did not; it has no resemblance of me; for if so, then indeed I might be considered "a military chieftain," as has been charged. I am, with great respect, your most obedient servant, Andrew Jackson . Messrs. Robert P. Henry, T.P. Moore, J.T Johnson, C.A. Wickliffe.

From the Commentator. Statement of the case of my counsel. I employed certain persons to build me a house, of particular dimensions and description, which they finished and I received, being well pleased with it. Since which, by some means, the house got infested with fleas, and I employed the same persons to cleanse it of those vermin, by brushing, washing, or fumigation, expressly (omitting the word only.) when meeting with some difficulty in doing it in that way, do you think the rascals did not burn down the house to kill the fleas? And when I reminded them of my restrictions to the modes mentioned in the compact, they had the effrontery to tell me they built the house, and consequently have a right to destroy it, and offer as precedent the re-organization act, which removes the judges from office, without the concurrence of two thirds as prescribed by the constitution, for (they say) as there is nothing in the constitution expressly forbidding the removal in any other way, so there was nothing in my compact with them to drive out the fleas by washing, brushing or fumigation which expressly forbids it being done by burning the house. I want to know if they have such a right and if not, what must be done with such wicked rascals, I am of the first water, A constitutional Judge Breaker.

By a treaty, says the National Journal, concluded at Washington on the 20th January, 1825, between the United States & the Choctaw nation of Indians, and ratified on the 19th ult. The Choctaws have agreed to cede to the United States all that portion of land ceded to them by the second article of the treaty of Doak Stand, lying east of a line beginning on the Arkansas, one hundred paces east of Fort Smith, and running thence, due south to Red River, it being understood that the line shall constitute and remain the permanent boundary between the United States and said nation; and the United States agreeing to remove such citizens as may be settled on the

The Mirror, Washington Kentucky   The Eagle, Maysville, Kentucky

west side to the east side of said line, and prevent future settlements from being made west thereof. The United States, in consideration of such cession, and on certain conditions agree to pay them 6,000 dollars annually forever.

Married on the Thursday evening last, by the Rev. J. T. Edgar, Mr. Hugh French to Miss Melinda Wilkinson, both of this vicinity.

Died in this town, last evening Mr. Joseph Coulter, at an advanced age.

POCKET BOOK LOST. Lost on Thursday last, the 1th inst. In the town of Maysville, a RED MOROCCO POCKET BOOK, with a steel clasp, containing about one dollar in currency, together with the following bonds: - Three on Benjamin Hart for $108 each, one due in the fall of 1825, one in 1826 and the other in 1827, also, one on the same individual for $67 1-3 due in January or February 1826; Colonel George Matthews and Philip Palmer securities: Also, one bond on James Shy and John Morford, due in April or May next, for 100 dollars - all of the above notes are for gold or silver. Also one now on demand on Enoch M. Tilton for $90. The person who may have found said book, will oblige the subscriber by returning it to him in Maysville, as the contents (save the little money it contains, to which he is welcome) can be of no use to any other person. John Robertson. Maysville, March 16, 1825

PUBLIC SALE. I will offer for sale, at the house of Ezekiel Beasley, Dec'd on Wednesday the 23d instant, the following property, to wit. HORSES, COWS, HOGS, SHEEP, one set of cooper's tools and sundry articles for agriculture. Also, to rent, the farm, belonging to the estate of E. Beasly, dec'd, including the Warehouse, &c., Also to hire, A Negro Man and Woman. Sale to commence at 10o'clock A.M. for all sums over five dollars, bond and security, payable in three months, required; under five dollars, payable in hand. L.L. Hawes, Administrator. Maysville, March 16, 1825

Juniata iron. The subscriber takes the liberty of informing the public, that he has commenced the manufacture of Iron into its various shapes, at his Juniata iron works in Pittsburgh, namely: common Bar Iron; Plough Plates; Waggon Tire of al sizes: Square, Round, Boiler, Sheet, Nail Iron and Nails, which he will sell on the lowest terms. As he manufactures the best Juniata Iron, he will stamp every bar 'P Shoenberger, Juniata Iron,' and his nails he will brand 'P Shoenberger, Juniata Nails, warranted.' He

<u>The Mirror, Washington Kentucky   The Eagle, Maysville, Kentucky</u>

will warrant the quality of his iron and Nails, to be inferior to none on the market Orders for Iron of the above description, and Nails, forwarded to this establishment, will be   promptly attended to. Peter Shoenberger. Juniata Iron Works, Pittsburgh

Maysville Fire Company. At the late election of officers of the Maysville Fire Company, the following persons were elected. Joseph Conwell, Captain; Cyrus Sanderson, First Lieutenant; P. H. Baird, Second Lieutenant; John Chambers, Engineer; W. Tinker, 1st Sergeant; R.C. Lilleston, 2d Sergeant; H. I. de Bruin, 3d Sergeant; and Henry C. Tureman 4th Sergeant. Supervisors for Upper Ward - P. Grant, M. Langhorne and John Armstrong. For Lower Ward Amos Corwine, Wm. Sutherland and Johnston Armstrong

Notice. This is to forewarn all persons from harboring or trusting my wife Hannah, as she has eloped from my bed and board, without any just cause, and I am determined to pay no debts of her contracting after this date. James Lawson. Greenup County, KY March 9, 1825

Greenup County Feb. 25, 1825 To whomever these presents shall come, greeting: We, John Mackoy and Moses Fuquee, pursuant to a special call of Sister Hannah Lawson, met at the house of brother James Lawson, and after hearing her complaint against said James, admitting it to be true, we think there was nothing in it worthy of notice, or any thing in it like a charge. And hearing both stories, with questions and the answers we are of opinion that the said Hannah has treated the old brother with too much contempt. Given under our hands, John Mackoy and Moses Fuquee.

Three pair of saddle bags lost. The friend who lately borrowed my saddlebags, will have the goodness to return them, as I have been deprived of the use of them fore sometime, and am now much in want of them. Two other pair have been loaned for nearly three years. If the persons who borrowed them, think they have them long enough, they will also be so kind as to return them. Each pair has my name written on the underside of the flap; and one pair has an outside pocket on each end. David Morrison. Maysville, March 2, 1825.

Storage and Commission Business, at Pittsburgh.   The undersigned respectfully informs Merchants and others, that he has recommenced the Storage and Commission Business, in the city of Pittsburgh. His warehouse is situated a few doors from Cromwell's old stand, on Wood

The Mirror, Washington Kentucky   The Eagle, Maysville, Kentucky

street, near the river. Being determined to devote the most unwearied attention to the business he respectfully solicits the custom of his friends and the public. A. M. Laughlin. Pittsburgh, January 16, 1825. Reference. Nat. Poyntz & Co., Maysville.

Literature. H. White, respectfully informs his friends, and the citizens generally of Maysville & its vicinity that he will open an English School, on Tuesday, the 1st of March, in the old Methodist church, lately occupied by Mr. and Miss Mollyneaux, for the reception of students, at the following prices per quarter: For Orthography, Reading & Writing $2.50, For Arithmetic, Grammar and Geography, $3.00. For Surveying, $6.00. Each student will pay an equal proportion of contingent expenses. Maysville, 23d Feb. 1825

Weaving. The subscriber has removed to his father's on Jersy Ridge, where he is prepared to weave. Double & Single Coverlets, of all kinds, in a style which cannot fail to please those who may employ him. R. Ricketts, Jn. Mason county, Oct. 14, 1824

Pittsburgh and Philadelphia line of Mail coaches, new arrangement. The attention of travelers going East and West, is hereby particularly invited. The proprietors of this ine have at the solicitation of may of their fellow citizens, determined to increase the running of their coach from Pittsburgh via Huntington, Lewistown and Harrisburgh, to three times per week, in less than four days each trip. They being met at the latter place by three different lines of stages, on the same evening - one running by way of Reading, and one by Lancaster, to Philadelphia and one other, via Little York to Baltimore. Travellers will not only get on with as much facility, but they will have choice of routes from Harrisburgh, which will at least afford variety. Every possible attention will be paid to their accommodation and their fare and traveling expenses generally made as low as on any other state route to Pennsylvania. The owners cannot be accountable for baggage. Rates of Fare, from Pittsburgh to Harrisburgh $10.00 (for any intermediate distance, six cents per mile. From Harrisburgh to Philadelphia $6.50. This line will call for passengers at any public or private house, at either end of the line, and will also drive to any place within reasonable distance, to let out gentlemen or ladies with their baggage. It will leave the hotels of Col. Ramsay in Pittsburgh, and Mrs. Buehler in Harrisburgh, respectively, on the mornings of Tuesday, Thursdays and Saturdays. Jno. Blair & others. February 4, 1825.

The Mirror, Washington Kentucky   The Eagle, Maysville, Kentucky

100 dollars reward. Stop the thief!!! Supposed to have been stolen from the subscriber living in Lewis County, on the waters of Cabin Creek, on Monday, the 7th instant, a Negro Woman & 3 Children. The woman is about 26 years of age, and has a large scar on her neck- the eldest girl is quite black, and about 7 years old- the second is a bright mulatto, 5 years old - the youngest is a boy 20 month old. The woman and child had on pale red dresses when they went away. I will give $50 reward, if the said Negroes are taken in this state and delivered to me, or $100 if taken out of the state. Geo. Rea Lewis County, K. March 9.

Land for sale. The subscriber offers for sale 180 acres of land, lying upon the North Fork of Licking, about 8 miles in an Eastern direction from Washington, and nearly the same distance from Maysville. There are between 60 and 70 acres of cleared land, under a good fence; the balance is a well timbered as any land in the country. On this farm, are good springs, a comfortable dwelling house, and out houses, and a thriving young orchard. For terms, apply to the subscriber. James Shackleford. Mason County, Feb. 2, 1825

Doctor Nelson, Tenders his professional services to the citizens of Maysville and its vicinity. He can be consulted at his office, on second street, in Armstrong's Row . Maysville, April, 7, 1824

APPROVED FAMILY MEDICINES. Which are celebrated for the cure of most diseases that the human frame is subject to . Prepared only by the sole proprietor, T.W.Dyott, MD Grandson of the late celebrated Dr. Robertson, of Edinburgh. And for sale, wholesale and retail, at his Drug and Family Medicine Warehouse, Nos. 137 and 139, north east corner of Second and Race streets, Philadelphia; and retail by his Agents and every principal Druggist and Vender of medicine throughout the United States. Where may be had, gratis, pamphlets either in English, German, French or Spanish, describing the qualities of each Medicine, with certificates of cures performed &c.,   Dr. Robetson's (sic) celebrated Stomach Elixir of Health - for the cure of coughs, colds, approaching consumption, hooping cough, asthma, pains in the breast, wind in the stomach, dyspepsia, bowel complaints , dysentery, &c.   Price $1.50 per bottle. Dr. Robertsons's Vegetable Nervous Cordial, or Nature's Grand Restorative - Recommended for the sure of nervous complaints generally, inward weakness, depression of the spirits, head ache, tremor, faintness, hysteric fits, nervous debility, intemperance, mercuriat disease, impotency, diseases peculiar to females, & c. Price $1.50 cents per bottle. Dr. Robertson's celebrated Gout and

The Mirror, Washington Kentucky The Eagle, Maysville, Kentucky

Rheumatic Drops. A sale and effectual cure for the gout, rheumatism, lumbago, stone and gravel, swellings and weakness of the joints, sprains, bruises, pains in the head & face, frosted feet, &c. Price $2 per bottle. Dr. Robertston's Stomachic Bitters - Celebrated for strengthening a weak stomach increasing the appetite, and certain preventive against the fever and ague, & c- Price one dollar per bottle. Dr. Robertson's Infallible Worm Destroying Lozenges. A medicine universally esteemed for expelling every species of worms from the human body. Price 50 cents per package; large packages $1.Dr. Dyott's Patent itch Ointment- For pleasantness, safety, expedition and certainty of cure, is unequaled by any other medicine in use for the removal of this disagreeable, tormenting complaint. It has no unpleasant smell, and may be used on the youngest infant with safety. Price 50 cents per box. Dr. Dyott's Infallible Tooth Ache Drops. Price 50 cents, small vials 25 cents. Dr. Dyott's Anti-Bilious Pills, which, if administered in time to remove the bile from the stomach, will prevent all bilious complaints, malignant fevers, ague and fever, bilious cholic, pleurisy, worms, dysentery, head ache, heart burn, loss of appetite, colds and coughs, dyspepsia or indigestion, habitual costiveness, &c. Price 25 cents per box, large boxes 50 cents. Dr. Vicker's Ointment for the cure of the Tetter, Ring Worm, & c. price 37 1-2 cents per box. Dr. Vicker's Embrocation for the Rheumatism, &c. Price 37 1-2 cents per bottle. Dr. Godbold's Vegetable Balm of Life - Price $1 per bottle Balm of Iberia. Extracted from an Iberian fragrant plant, for removing defects of the skin and improving the complexion- price $2 per bottle. The Restorative Dentrifice. For cleansing, whitening and preserving the teeth and gums. Price 50 cents per box. The Circassian eye Water: Celebrated for curing most disorders of the Eyes - Price 50 cents, small vials 25 cents. Mahy's Approved Plaster Cloth: A sovereign remedy for all ulcers and sores, sore breast, boils, sore legs, swellings, sprains, cuts, bruises, pains in the back and breast, corns on the feet, &c: Price 25 cents, 50 cents and $1 for each size plaster. Approved and recommended by Dr. Rush and Dr. Physick, of Philadelphia, and by the most eminent of the faculty in the U.S. Take notice, that in order to prevent imposition, all and each of the above genuine medicines are neatly sealed up with full directions for using them, and signed on the outside covers with the signature of the sole proprietor, T.W. Dyott; MD Since the introduction of these valuable medicines into the U.S. of America, they have acquired the highest degree of celebrity for their unparalleled success in alleviating and curing diseases, which, in a variety of instances, had baffled some of our most experienced physicians. The extensive and increasing demand for them throughout the continent, for these twenty years past, testifies their interesting efficacy and

The Mirror, Washington Kentucky   The Eagle, Maysville, Kentucky

importance to the public. For families and individuals whose residence or circumstances place them beyond the advantage of procuring a physician, they are peculiarly adapted; and for those convenience they are accompanied with every instruction appertaining to the symptoms of diseases, and proper directions for using them. A considerable discount will be made to Druggist, Country Merchants, and those who purchase by the quantity. Orders promptly attended to and the medicines carefully packed and forwarded to any part agreeable to direction. Dec. 15-13A fresh supply of the above Medicines just received and for sale by John Armstrong, Maysville.

Platt Stout, (Late of Maysville, Ken) has removed to Florence Alabama, for the purpose of carrying on a General Storage and commission business. He respectfully offers his services to merchants and planters in the sale of western produce; in the receiving and forwarding of merchandise, and in the sale, purchase or shipping of cotton, and the agency of any business that may be entrusted to his management. His sales room at present, is on the west side of the public square, in the white house lately occupied by Mrs. Hagaty: He trust, by uniting strict attention and persevering industry to the knowledge which more than seven years' experience as a Commission Merchant, has necessarily afforded, to give entire satisfaction to those who may commit their business to his management. Being nearly a stranger in Alabama, he respectfully submits, as references, a few of his commercial friends, in different points, who will afford any information in relation to him, as a man of business.   Messrs. Jno. Simpson & Co. Messrs. Black & Webb,. Mr. George Boggs, Jr. Florence Al   Messrs. Malone & Metcalfe, Huntsville, Mr Thomas Yeatman, Wm. G. Hunt, Esq. Nashville, TN. Florence, October 1824.

Law Notice. Mason Brown, Attorney at Law, will hereafter regularly attend the Mason, Lewis and Bracken circuit courts; and also the court of common pleas, in Brown county, Ohio His office is on Front Street, one door above the post office. Maysville, March 2, 1824.

ONE HUNDRED DOLLARS REWARD. Ran away from the farm of A.K. Alexander, in the county of Franklin and the state of Kentucky, a Mulatto man slave named GEORGE. The property of A. K. Marshall. George was hired to said Alexander, and some quarrel having taken place with the overseer, he absconded, about the 19th of November, 1823. He is a light mulatto, formerly be longed to the estate of Violett, who by his will devised him free; but said Violett being in debt, George was sold under execution,

The Mirror, Washington Kentucky   The Eagle, Maysville, Kentucky

and purchased by J. J. Marshall of the town of Frankfort. George is about 5 feet 9 or 10 inches high, has a slight, genteel person, a brisk intelligent countenance: But he can be identified beyond dispute, by a scar which has deprived him of all hair on a large part of his head. He wears his hair long, and attempts to conceal the scar by combing it smooth over it. He has probably a copy of Violett' will with him, and passes as free; but he is a slave, as above stated. He has been seen in the steam boat Maise, and probably continues in it. The above reward will be paid upon delivery of said George, in Frankfort, to the subscriber or by confining him in jail at Maysville (Washington) or Louisville, so that he come to the possession of the subscriber. J.J. Marshall. Frankfort Aug. 21 1824

Storage and Commission Business. The subscribers continue to transact the storage and commission business at their stand on Second Street, where they offer for sale the following articles, viz: Copperas, by the keg, half barrel or barrel. Glass Ware, assorted. Nails. Iron Wire Seives, Coffee, by the bag. Patent Ploughs. Window Glass, assorted. Buffalo Robes. Logwood. New Orleans Sugar. Gin, by the keg. Cordial, by the keg. Bounce, by the keg. Bonnet Boards. Writing Paper, Nos. 1,2, &3. Wrapping Paper, different sizes. Tin Ware, assorted. Together with a variety of other articles, which will be sold low for cash or bartered for Hemp, Beeswax, Feathers, or such other produce as may suit the market. January & Sutherland. Maysville, Jan 12, 1825.

Doctor Shackleford, Having recently removed to Maysville, offers his professional services to the citizens of the town and the surrounding country. He may always be found, unless absent on professional business, at his office on Water street, next door to Mr. D. Morrison's store, or at Captain Langhorne's tavern. Maysville, April 7, 1824

Anna Beard: Take Notice - that on the 23d day of April next, at the office of L. L. Hawes, Maysville, KY. I shall proceed to take sundry depositions to be used as evidence in a suit in chancery for divorce, now depending in the Mason circuit court, in which I am complainant and you are respondent. Arthur Beard. March 9, 1825

Storage and Commission Business. The subscriber respectfully begs leave to inform his friends and customers, that he still continues the storage and commission business, as usual, at his stand two doors below the post Office, on Water Street and has on hand a variety of Articles for sale, vix. Dearborn and Wagon Tire, rolled.

The Mirror, Washington Kentucky   The Eagle, Maysville, Kentucky

Bowen's best 3, 4, 6, 8 and 10d nails and Brads.
Phoenix " 8 and 10d do do
Common 4, 6, 8 and 10d Nails & Brads
8 by 10 and 10 by 12 Gen. Window Glass
Sheet IRON
3 hoop do
A general assortment of PAPER
A few sacks best GREEN COFFEE
Together with a variety of other articles, which he will sell low for Cash, or barter for good FEATHERS, Leaf TOBACCO in hogsheads, BEEXWAX, Clean Linen and Cotton RAGS, or such other articles as may suit the market. JOHN HALDEMAN. Maysville, Nov 3, 1824

Thomas Y. Payne, Attorney at Law, Having settled himself in Maysville, Kentucky will attend to the practice of his profession in the circuit and county courts of Mason and Bracken, and the circuit courts of Lewis and Fleming counties, Kentucky, and the superior courts in the county of Brown, Ohio.   His office is in the brick house owned by John T. Langhorne, corner of Main Cross and Second Streets. April 21, 1824

Iron Foundry. Having rented the Iron Foundry owned by the Messrs. Hewitts, in this town, for a term of time - we are prepared to fill al orders for castings, made to pattern, of every description, on the shortest notice and mot favorable terms. Swan & Starr. Maysville 29th Dec. 1824

BOOK STORE. Edward Cox, Book-binder, Respectfully informs his friends that he has removed to five doors higher up into the brick row on Front street; where has a good assortment of Books for sale on a reasonable terms as any in the western country.
E.C. has ledgers, Journals &c made of the best Philadelphia paper; also, Day Books, Records Books, Memorandums, Cyphering Books &c Blank Books of any kind made on the shortest notice. Old or New Books Bound in a neat and durable manner.
A good circulating library, consisting of Novels, Romances, Plays, Histories and Miscellaneous Books. The terms are 50 cents per month or 6 1-4 cents per volume for all of one dollar or less.
Family Bibles, elegant or plain - do with Schott or Cann's References. Scott's Family Bibles, 3 vols 4to.   School and Pocket Bibles and Testaments.
Hymn Books, by Dobell, Dwight, Dupuy, Watts, Wesley and Noel and Verdeman-Gardener's Christian Hymn Book.

The Mirror, Washington Kentucky   The Eagle, Maysville, Kentucky

Confession of Faith- Alen's History of the Reformation - milner's Church History- Buck's Theological Dictionary= Campbell and Maccalla's Debate on Baptism- Josephus, 3 vols. -Life of Jesus Christ.
Wesley's Platosophy 2 vols. Paley's philosophy- Stewart's philosophy of the mind. Ferguson's Astronomy, 3 vols. Do abridged - Reid's philosophy, 3 vol. Gibbon's Rome, 6 vols. Hume's England- Russell's Modern Europe- Plutarch's Lives- Plowden's Ireland - Edward's West Indies - Gillie's Greece- Welpley's Compend of History, Ancient and Modern.
Nicholson's Encyclopedia 12 vol.
Brooks Gazetter, with the Constitution of each state - Constitutions of all the United States $1.
Napoleon in Exile- Las Cases' Journal. Shakespeare's Plays, 8 vols.
Freemason's Monitor - Masonic Constitutions- Masonic Chart and Key to do.
Nation Militia Standard, 2 vol- Scott's Infantry Exercises- Duane's Hand Book for Infantry and Riflemen.
Freeman Lewis' Beauties of Harmony- Law's Harmonic companion - Metcalfe's Kentucky Harmonist _ Little & Smith, Wyeth and Adgate's Music Books.
Fifes, Flutes & Flagelets - Violin Strings
A pair of London made 12 inch Globes, with the latest discoveries, terrestrial and celestial, to 1821, with a book of instrucitons $45.00
Keith on the Globes - Simpson's Euclid's Elements - Bonnycastle's Algebra - Hunton's Course of Mathematices- Morse's and Guthries's Geopraphy, 2 vols each, with maps - Cumming's Geography and Atlas - Woodbridge's do – Adam's and Atlas - Smiley's Geography and beautiful Atlas- Smiliey's Sacred Atlas price 75 cents.
Latin and Greek School Books, of every kind in use.
Webster's American Spelling Book 12 1-2 cents each - do by the dozen or gross.   United States' spelling - Pickett's Juvenile Spelling - Smith's Defining Spelling.
Murray's introduction, English Reader & Sequel - Do. Grammar, Exercises ey.   Columbian Orator - Dialogues for Schools- Sandford and Merton - American Orator - American Preceptor - Goldsmith's History of England - Do. Rome and Greece.
Weems' Life of Marion and Washington- Life of Franklin, Penn, Decatur &c—History of the Late War. Letter Writers.
Clerk's and Magistrate's Assistant.
Walker's and Johnson's large and small Dictionaries - Arithmetics, by Daboil, Adams, Guthrie, Gough, Bennett, stockton, Jess, Walsh and Jyse - Pike's large and small arrithmetic Key to Pike and Bennett. Greenleaf's

The Mirror, Washington Kentucky   The Eagle, Maysville, Kentucky

Grammar simplified – Fint's Jess's Gibson's and Gummare's Surveying – Mathematical Instruments. Slates and Pencils - Camel's Hair Pencils - Crayon's black lead Pencils - Boxes of Water Colours - India Ink - Cards- Office Wafers - Backgammon Boxes - Dominos- Plain, fancy and gilt-edged Letter paper - Writing and Drawing papers of all sizes - Black and red Ink Powders - Quills - Gold Leaf.
Parkhurst's Greek Lexicon - Do. Hebrew - Ewell's Medical Companion- Buchan's Domestic Medicine.
A valuable collection of Medical Books for gentlemen of the faculty. Sept. 8, 1824

A Great and Useful Desideratum. Dr. Thomas O. Williams, of Maysville, Mason County, has discovered a chemical preparation, which proves to be an infallible cure for the tooth ache, it likewise preserves the gums and teeth from decay: and is a sovereign remedy for the Aphthae (or Thrash) in children. The medicine is perfectly mild and safe, and the necessary instructions for using will accompany it. At present it can only be had of the proprietor, or (in his absence) his family. Price 25 cents per box.

Printed and Published by Lewis Collins Sutton Street Maysville Terms Two dollars in advance; two dollars and fifty cents paid within the year or three dollars if not paid until the year expries, in specie or its equivalent; Advertising For one square, first three insertions one dollar - each subsequent insertion, 25 cents. Larger advertisements in proportion. A reasonable deduction will be allowed to those who advertise by the year

March 23, 1825

Public Sale. I will offer for sale, at the house of Ezekiel Beasley, dec'd on Wednesday the 23d instant, the following property, to wit: Horses, Cows, Hogs, Sheep. One set of Cooper's tools, and sundry articles for agriculture. Also, to rent, the farm. Belonging to the estate of E. Beasley dec'd including the warehouse & c. Also to hire, A Negro Man and Woman. Sale to commence at 10o'clock, A. M. For all sums over five dollars, bond and security, payable in three months, required, under five dollars, payable in hand. L. L. Hawes, administror, Maysville, March 16, 1825.

The Mirror, Washington Kentucky   The Eagle, Maysville, Kentucky

The Union of the 9th inst.; contains the speech of Robert Taylor, Esq. Delivered at the public meeting in Washington on the 26th ult. We shall, in the course of a few weeks, publish it in our columns.

A communication is received from Lewis County, in which a general meeting of the citizens of that county is requested at the house of Thomas Parker, Esq. On the second Tuesday in April, to express their sentiments on the re-organization of the court of appeals. The address shall appear next week.

We are authorized to announce ALEXANDER BRUCE, esq. As a candidate to represent the people of Lewis County in the next legislature

Desha's Trial. The second trial of Isaac B. Desha, commenced on Monday, the 14th instant, being the first day of the Harrison circuit court. On Thursday, no juryman having been obtained, we learned that the trial was laid over until the June Court.

In Bourbon About 200 persons met at Wm Moreland's tavern, in Bourbon, last week- and adopted, with but one dissenting voice, resolutions in opposition to the judge breaking act of the last legislature.

Bracken County. We copy the following from the commentator of the 19th inst. We hope that Captain Rudd will deem it his duty to tender his services to his county at this important crisis. Bracken county March 6, 1825. To Capt. Thomas Rudd: Sir, You have once represented us and we now call on you to offer your services again We wish to be represented by a man of firmness. We think we hold a claim on yon. We now think that our rights are infringed; and call on you to consent to represent us in the next general assembly. Many of the citizens of Bracken county.

Cam. Porter arrived at his residence near Washington city, on the 2d instant from Thompson's Island, whence he had been recalled.

Doctor Buchanan (says a late Louisville paper) succeeded yesterday in propelling a wagon some three or four miles, with a very small capillary steam engine. The experiment, we are informed succeeded beyond the most sanguine anticipation of its ingenious inventor.

A Philadelphia physician, in a letter to a lady on the deleterious effects of wearing corsets, has the following observations: "I anticipate the happy

The Mirror, Washington Kentucky   The Eagle, Maysville, Kentucky

period when the fairest portion of the fair creation will step forth unencumbered with slabs of walnut and tiers of whalebone. The constitutions of our females must be excellent to withstand, in any tolerable degree the terrible infliction of the corset eight long hours every day. No other animal could survive it. Take the honest ox, and enclose his sides with hoop poles, put an oaken plank beneath him, and gird the whole with a bed cord, and demand of him to labor; he would labor, indeed; but it would be for breath."

Mr. Thomas Edwards, of King William county, Virginia, was lately killed by his slaves. They separated his body into several parts with an axe and deposited them in different places. The slaves were arrested.

Golden luck. A wood-chopper lately found twenty-nine golden guineas in the trunk of a tree, which he felled in the woods near Utica. An augur hold had been bored into the tree, the gold deposited, plugged in, and the bark grown over the aperture.

Considerable interest, says the Manchester Guardian, has been excited in this town during the present week, by a visit from the Pacha of Egypt. The name of this extraordinary visitor is Ali Effendi; and it is stated to us that he fills a station in the court of the Pacha, somewhat analogous to that of grand chamberlain. From his title of Effendi, however, we should rather suppose that he is a secretary. We believe he was a Mameluke, and served in the capacity of aid de camp to Ibrahim, the son of the Pacha, when the Wechabites were driven from Mecca. We understand that he has been sent to this country for the purpose of studying its language, manners and institutions; and certainly, from what we have heard of his intelligence and acuteness, we should think that the Pacha could hardly have chosen a better agent.

Washington City, March 9. The treaty late concluded by the commissioners of the United States, on the one part, and the Creek Indians on the other, of the cession of lands lying within the limits of the state of Georgia has been confirmed by the senate.

Married - In Lexington, on the 10th instant, Mason Brown, Esq. Of Maysville, to Miss Judith Ann Bledsoe, daughter of the Hon. Jesse Bledsoe.

Bertrand (By the Celebrated OLD PRINTER,) I AM AUTHORIZED TO STATE, WILL STAND THE ENSUING SEASON AT Washington, Mason

The Mirror, Washington Kentucky   The Eagle, Maysville, Kentucky

county, in the stable occupied last season by the Virginia Whip. The season to commence on the 1st day of April. Bertrand is a beautiful mahogany bay, black legs, mane and tail, full sixteen hands, high and for beauty and symmetry of form, and of muscular power and action, is not surpassed by any horse in the state. He need only to be seen to recommend him to every gentleman who is desirous of breeding fine horses. Every necessary provision will be made for and care taken of, mares from a distance; but not accountability of accidents. Mr. Hamet, who kept Whip last season, is engaged to superintend Bertrand. For rates and to her particulars, see bills. Jno. N. Payne. March 23, 1825

Juniata Iron. Unreadable Advertisement by Peter Shoenberger.

Land for sale. The subscriber offers for sale 180 acres of land, lying upon the North Fork of Licking, about 8 miles in an eastern direction from Washington, and nearly the same distance from Maysville. There are between 60 and 70 acres of cleared land, under a good fence; the balance is well timbered as any land in the country. On the Farm, are good springs, a comfortable dwelling house, and out houses, and a thriving young orchard. For terms apply to the subscriber James Shackleford. Mason Co. February 2, 1825

The following is a list of non-resident's lands, as entered with the auditor of public Accounts, lying in Mason County, and the tax with interest due thereon, with the years thereto annexed.

Will be sold on the fourth Monday in October next, being court day, at the court house in Washington, for ready money . The above tracts of land, or so much of each tract as will be sufficient to satisfy the tax and interest due thereon for the above years. The sale to continue from day to day, until the whole is sold. N. B. At the same time I will purchase Auditors, Warrants & Claims. September 9th, 1799 James Dobyns, S. M. C. J.D.

Proprietors	land	rule	Water Course	For whom entered	For whom surveyed
Thomas Perkins,	12953	2	On licking	Tho. Perkins,	Tho. Perkins,
William Skillern,	2000	3	Waters of Sandy	W. Skellem	W. Skellem
James Primen,	100	2	Waters of Licking,		
Peter Burtoram,	1701	3	Little Sandy	Will. Woddy,	Will. Woddy,
Mathias Bryle,	50		Near Upper Blue-Lick,	M. Bryle,	M. Bryle,
John Hill,	16		Cabin Creek,	J. Marshall,	
Archibald Wood	80		Ohio	A. Woods,	A. Woods,
Ditto,	604	2	Lees Creek, head of first right branch	Ditto,	Ditto,
John & James Perry	100		Near May's Lick	J & J Perry	J & J Perry
Ditto,	1000		Mill Creek,	Ditto,	Ditto,
Thomas F. Bates,	410	3	Licking,	T.F. Bates,	T.F. Bates,
Charles Morgan	46		Lawrence's Creek Waters,	Charles Morgan	Charles Morgan
James Elliott,	68		on Licking	Elliott & others,	Elliott & others,
Joseph Moore,	4000		north Fork of Licking,	J. Moore,	J. Moore,
George Moore	1000		Ditto	George Moore,	George Moore,
David Patterson,	5000		Salt-Lick Creek		
Richard Moore,	400		Fox (?) Creek,	R. Moore,	
John Haworth,	7000		Branch of North Fork of Sandy River		
Walter Brame,	1500			W. Brame,	W. Brame,
John & James M'Alexander & others	50			J. M'Alexander and (J. M'Alexander and o
Joseph Watkins,	50		Flemings Fork of Licking	Joseph Watkins,	Joseph Watkins,
Thomas Watkins,	20		Licking		
Ditto,	60		Ditto,		
John Cundiff	100		Locust Creek,	J. Cundiff,	J. Cundiff
William Nelson,	100		Cabin Creek,	W. Nelson	W. Nelson
John Odaniel,	270		north Fork of Licking,		
Francis West,	537		Waters of Salt-Lick Creek,	J. Fowler,	
Ditto,	500		Tygers Creek,	Ditto,	
Walter Ford	1000		Licking,		
Samuel Brackman	500		Ditto,		
Joshua Jones	250		North Fork of Licking, Wednesday September 4, 1799		

Proprieters	land	rule Water Course	For whom entered	For whom surveyed
Cary L. Clarke,	1819	Waters of Sandy,		
Charles Yancy,	1000	Waters of Ohio,	Thomas Tharpe,	Thomas Tharpe,
George Barnette,	5000	North Fork of Licking,	G. Barnette,	G. Barnette,
Ditto & Jo. Davis	1560	Little Sandy river,	J. Davis,	J. Davis,
Tilman Weaver,	74	Ditto,	T. Weaver,	T. Weaver,
George Rice,	66	Waters of Licking,		
Reubin Austin,	1000	North Fork waters,	F. Austin,	F. Austin,
Henry Timberlake,	1000	ditto,	Ditto,	Ditto,
John Patrick,	258	Licking,		
Ditto	250	Ten miles from Lower Blue Lick,		F. McConnel,
Ditto,	250	Six Ditto,		Ditto
Ditto,	250	Lawrance's Creek,		
Ditto,	250	Ditto, first large branch of Ditto,		
Nicholas Watkins,	1000	Water of Ohio,	Ditto,	Ditto,
Ditto,	500	Ditto,		
Ditto,	4000	Ditto,		
John Watkins,	3500	Ditto,		
Ditto	3400	Ditto,		
Ditto,	4000	Ditto,		
Ditto,	4000	Ditto,		
Robert Watkins,	4000	Ditto,		
Ditto,	3500	Ditto,		
William Walker,	2000	Waters of Licking,	W. Walker	W. Walker
Ditto, junr.	2000	Ditto,	Ditto,	Ditto,
William Glaves,	562	Joining Kincaid's		
William Eve,	13000	Kinnacanick Creek,	M. Walker	M. Walker
Tench Coxe,	8000		H. L. Charton	H. L. Charton
Thomas Follis	1000	North Fork of Licking,	T. Follis	F. Foushee,
Matthew Gayle,	200	Joining May's Lick,	M. Gayle,	M. Gayle,
Ditto.	400	Ditto,	Ditto,	Ditto,
John Gayle,	600	North Fork of Licking,	J. Gayle,	J. Gayle,
Wade Mosby	5767	Johnston's Fork,	J. Mosby,	L. Mosby

Wednesday September 4, 1799

100

Proprieters	For whom patented	Years due							Amount		
		92	93	94	95	96	97	98	E	s	D
Thomas Perkins,		2	3	4	5	6	7	8	2	14	8
William Skillern,	W. Skellern						7	8			8
James Primen,					5	6	7			?	8
Peter Burtoram,	Will. Woddy,						7				
Mathias Bryle,	M. Bryle,						7				
John Hill,											
Archibald Wood	A. Woods,							8			
Ditto,	Ditto,							8			
John & James Perry	J & J Perry							8			
Ditto,	Ditto,							8			
Thomas F. Bates,	T.F. Bates,						7				
Charles Morgan	Charles Morgan							8			
James Elliott,	Elliott & others,							8			
Joseph Moore,	J. Moore,						7	8			
George Moore	G. Moore,	2	3	4	5			8	2		2
David Patterson,									2		4
Richard Moore,										7	5
John Haworth,											3
Walter Brame,	W. Brame,										9
John & James M'Ale	J. M'Alexander and others										
Joseph Watkins,	J. Watkins,										6
Thomas Watkins,											6
Thomas Watkins,											6
John Cundiff	J. Cundiff	2	3	4	5	6	7			7	4
William Nelson,	W. Nelson	2	3	4	5	6	7				6
John Odaniel,										7	4
Francis West,									2	9	4
Ditto,		2	3	4		6			3	3	4
Walter Ford			3	4			7		14		10
Samuel Brackman			3	4					2	11	2
Joshua Jones	S. Brackman,		3	4			7				1
										101	

Wednesday September 4, 1799

Name	For whom patented	Years							Amount		
Cary L. Clarke,	R Craddock,	2	3	4				8	##	94	4
Charles Yancy,	C. Fleming,							8		5	9
George Barnette,	Assigned to Yancy,							8		3	10
Ditto & Jo. Davis	O. Barnette,	2	3	4				8	14		3
Tilman Weaver,	Ditto & Davis, T.	2	3	4				8	4	7	9
George Rice,	T. Weaver,							8		3	8
Reubin Austin,	Rice Assignee Harris					7		8	1	4	
Henry Timberlake,	T. Austin,			5	6	7		8	1	1	
John Patrick,	Ditto			5	6	7		8	1	1	
John Patrick,								8			11
John Patrick,								8			2
John Patrick,	F. M'Connell,				6	7		8		4	
John Patrick,	Ditto,				6	7		8		4	
Nicholas Watkins,			3	4		6	7	8	2	16	2
Nicholas Watkins,			3	4			7	8			7
Nicholas Watkins,							7			11	
John Watkins,											9
John Watkins,							7		1	8	8
John Watkins,									1	8	8
John Watkins,										8	8
Robert Watkins,		2	3		5	6				8	7
Robert Watkins,		2	3	4	5	6	7			16	7
William Walker,	W. Walker									7	6
Ditto, junr.	Ditto,									7	6
William Glaves,										2	1
William Eve,	M. Walker								2	8	9
Tench Coxe,	H. L. Charton	2	3	4	5	6	7		1	10	6
Thomas Follis,	F. Foushee,	2	3	4	5	6	7		1	2	4
Matthew Gayle,	M. Gayle,	2	3	4	5	6	7	8	5	12	6
Ditto,	Ditto,	2	3	4	5	6	7	8	1	2	6
John Gayle,	J. Gayle,	2	3	4	5	6	7	8	1	2	6
Wade Mosby,	L. Mosby	2	3	4	5	6	7	8	16	4	6

Wednesday September 4, 1799

The Mirror, Washington Kentucky   The Eagle, Maysville, Kentucky

A
Abbott
　Isaac............ 58
ADAMS
　John Quincy,
　　President. 85
　Spencer........ 71
Addison
　Alexander.... 13
　Mr................ 14
　Thos............. 43
Ailles
　Richard........ 58
Albertson
　Uriah........... 47
Alexander
　A. K............. 93
　James........... 65
Alison
　Andrew........ 44
Allen
　Col................. 6
　John.............. 46
　Nath................ 5
Allot
　Rev. Mr. Brian 7
Amburgh
　Benjamin..... 54
　Betsy............ 54
Anderson
　Achsa........... 43
　C.V............... 74
　Stokes........... 61
Applegate
　Richard........ 43
Ardreett
　Henry........... 43
Armer
　John............. 58

Armstrong
　James . 6, 13, 18
　Jno................ 72
　John 38, 67, 68, 72, 88, 92
　Johnson........ 66
　Johnston. 74, 88
　William 6, 13, 18
Arnold
　Henry........... 58
　Lewis H........ 66
Ashly
　William........ 23
Atherton
　Caleb............ 58
Atkinson
　Wm............... 58
Austain
　James........... 12
Austin
　F. 102
　Reubin 102, 104
　T. 104
Avery
　Bela............. 76
　Mr................ 64

B
Baddolet
　John............. 43
Badgley
　Andrew........ 43
Bahr
　Thos. T......... 78
Bailey
　James........... 43
Bailor
　Col................. 5
Baird
　P.H............... 88
　Pleasant H.... 59

Baker
　John............. 43
Baldwin
　James........... 41
　Jane.............. 65
　Samuel... 41, 65
Ballard
　William........ 35
Ballenger
　Susan........... 78
Ballingal
　David........... 28
Bannon
　James........... 76
Barber
　David . 4, 10, 18
Barker
　Mr................ 53
　Robert.... 16, 53
Barnes
　Blacsslee...... 59
Barnette
　G. 102
　George 102, 104
　O. 104
Barrett
　John............. 44
Barry
　Chief Justice 82
Bartlet & Cox, .. 80
Bartram
　S.A............... 59
Barwell
　Nicholas....... 59
BATES
　A. 70
　Thomas F.101, 103
Baxter
　Edmund........ 30
Beall

103

The Mirror, Washington Kentucky   The Eagle, Maysville, Kentucky

Benjamin 23
George M. ... 82
Beals
   Robert, Major 23
Bean
   Phantley R. ... 59
Bear
   Thomas 59
Beard
   Anna 94
   Arthur 94
Beasley
   Ezekiel ... 87, 97
   John 23
   N. 81
   Nathaniel 76, 79
BEASLY
   N. 61
Beaumont
   W. H. 6, 22
   W.H. 17, 49
   Wm. M. 44
Bee
   Judge 51
Beggs
   Hannah 79
   John 79
Bell
   Umphrey 59
   William 2
Belton
   Joseph 9
Berry
   Samuel 23
Bett
   Mersham 50
Bibb
   Charles S. 82
Black
   Black & Webb. 92
   Rudolph 43

Black Feet Indians 63
Blackburn
   Benjamin 30
Blair
   Francis P. 82
   Jno. 90
Blanchard
   John 59
Bland
   Lewis 64
Blandchard
   D. 43
Bledsoe
   Jesse, Hon. ... 99
   Judith Ann. ... 99
Bodley
   Thomas .. 20, 78
Bodley,
   Thomas .. 19, 20
Bogges
   Thomas 74
Boggs
   George 92
Boon
   Jacob 24
Bowman
   Benj. 59
Boyd
   John 55, 63
Brackenridge
   Mr. 14
   Robert 23
Brackman
   S. 103
   Samuel 101, 103
BRAGG
   Tho. 73
Brame
   Walter 101, 103
Bravard
   Adam 23

Brawner
   Ignatious 59
Brazel
   James 35
Brewer
   Edward 59
BRICK
   Ephraim 72
BRIDGES
   Lewis 60
Briely
   Thomas 59
Brittingham
   Purnel 59
Broadwell
   Samuel 23
Brodrick
   David .5, 43, 48
Bronaugh
   William 32
Broner
   Boas 59
Broohover
   Asael 23
Brookes's
   Wm. 44
Brooks
   William B. 56
Brough
   Peter 31
Brown
   Grier 23
   James 43
   Jinks 59
   John 36, 72
   John, Capt. 17, 42
   John, Maj. 69
   Joseph 43, 45
   Mason 93, 99
   Wm. Dr. 76
BRUCE

The Mirror, Washington Kentucky The Eagle, Maysville, Kentucky

Alexander 97
Bruin, de
  H.I. 88
Bryle
  Mathias 101, 103
Bryma
  Bailey 74
Buchanan
  Doctor 98
  James 43
Buckner
  Wil. 83
Buehler
  Mrs. 90
Bullock
  Lewis 23
Burgess
  Basil 43
Burke
  Mr. 13
Burley
  Phill 25
Burris
  Matthew 74
Burtoram
  Peter .. 101, 103
Butt
  William.. 59, 75
BYERS
  E.G. 69
  J. 69

C

Cable
  Mr. 3
Caldwell
  Rebecca 23
  Silas 59
  Wm. 79
Callaway
  Edmund 22

Campbell
  Evan 59
  James 43, 44
  Jjames C. 59
  Robert 19
Campsey
  Wm. 59
Cararan
  Barney 23
Carneal
  Thos. D. 79
Carrell
  Mr. 64
Carter
  Thomas 59
Carye
  Ludwell 59
Case,
  Mr. Loudon .. 15
Cassiday
  Michael 24
Casto
  Abijam 78
Chain
  Thomas 24
Chamberlain
  John 75
Chambers
  James 60
  Jno. 66
  John 88
  Mr. 67
Chapin
  Lucius 55
Chapman
  Henry 23
  John S. 82
Charton
  H.L. ... 102, 104
Chickasaws 35
Chinn

Raweigh 11
Rawleigh 17, 18
Choctaws 87
Clark
  Joseph 44
  Thomas 59
Clarke
  Cary L.102, 104
Clay
  Henry 78
  Mr. 3
Claybrok
  Disa 59
Clayten
  Mr. 53
Clayton
  William 23
Cleneay
  William 37
Cleveland
  Mr. 53
Cloud
  C.W., Rev. 78
Clymer
  George 20
Coburn
  John .56, 59, 79
Cochran
  Andrew 23
  John 59
Coffe
  Isaac 35
Colberison
  Robert 59
Coleman
  Robert 43
Collins
  Edward 23
  Eli 43
  Lewis 96
Combelt

Jacob 24
Combest
  Carral 23
Compton
  Richard .. 43, 52
Comton
  Elizabeth 53
  Jacob 53
Conwell
  Joseph 88
Cooper
  John 44
  Murdock 49
Cord
  Acquila 23
Cordingley
  Wm. 59
Corwine
  Amos, Jr. 62
  Amose 88
Cosse
  Isaac 35
Cotwine
  Amos 62
Coulter
  James 59
  Joseph 87
Cowan
  G. 78
COX
  Edward 95
  Nath'l 68, 80
Coxe
  Tench. 102, 104
Craddock
  R. 104
Craig
  Elizabeth 30
  Lewis 20, 59
  William 30
Crain

Robert A. 59
Crane
  James 43
  John, Col. 23
  Samuel 43
  Creek Indians ... 50
Criswell
  Robert 34
Crittenden
  John J 82
  Mr. 82
Cromwell 89
Crookshank, R. 65
Crosby
  William 12
Crosby.
  William 3
Cummings
  Wm. 59
Cundiff
  John ... 101, 103
Currey
  James 23, 44
Curtis
  Mr. 64
Cushing
  Mr. 45

D

Dabney
  Nathaniel
    Gardner ... 55
Daconigait
  Mr. 27
Dalce
  Bazil 79
Dale
  Charles ... 24, 44
DANIEL
  James 71
Dart

Jonathan 59
DAULTON
  George W. 61
Davis
  F.A.W.H. 83
  J. 102
  James 59
  Jo. 102, 104
  John 59
  Joseph 59
  Mr. 3
  Samuel 80
  T. 104
Dawson
  Robert D. 59
de Bruin
  H.I. 88
Delana
  Joseph 21
Delando
  Stephen 64
Delano
  Stephen, jr. ... 64
Dennison
  Timothy 59
Denny
  Jas. W. 78
DEPEW
  Alexander R. 69
Depuy
  Abraham 59
Desfourneaux
  Gen. 7
Desha
  Isaac B. 97
  Joseph 12, 31
Devour
  Henry 59
Dibell
  William 38
Dill

The Mirror, Washington Kentucky   The Eagle, Maysville, Kentucky

John 9
Soloman 24
Dillon
  James 59
Disbrow
  Hen. 21
Dobyns
  Edward 41
  James 23, 31
Doggott
  Elmore 44
Donathan
  Anderson 59
Dones
  Mr. 29
Dones and Sinclair 29
Dougharty
  Michael,
    Doctor 44
Dougherty
  John 40
DOYLE
  Charles 67
Drake
  Abraham 20
Dudley
  William 50
Duke
  James R. 59
  Thomas M. ... 79
Duncan
  Ennis, Jun'r. . 75
Duval
  J.P. 43
Dye
  Margaret 44
Dyott
  T.W., M.D. 90

E

Eagle Office 80

EASTON
  Edward 67
Edgar
  J.T., Rev. 87
Editor
  Aurora 32
Editor of the
  Aurora 6
Editors of the
  Mirror 42
Edwards
  Amos 48
  John 10
  John, Col 24
  John, Sen. 18, 23
  John, Senr. ... 48
  Thomas, Mr. 98
Effendi
  Ali 98
Elder
  John 24
Eldridge
  John 24
Ellicot
  Mr. 2, 7
Ellicott
  Mr. 51
Elliot
  Resin 59
Elliott
  James . 101, 103
Ellis
  Duddley B. .. 59
  Elizabeth 59
  Jesse 59
  John 81
  Lucinda 59
Ellis' Ferry 70
English
  Chester 59
Evans

Mr. 3
Eve
  William 102, 104
Ewell
  Bertrand . 11, 18
  Jesse 11, 18

F

F. SHULTZ
  HIXSON & Co 69
Faris
  James 50
Farror
  John 59
Feizer
  philip 78
Felix
  Citoyen 53
Ficklia
  James 59
Ficklin
  Joseph K. 80
Field
  Henry 35, 40
  Mrs 35
Findley
  John E., Revd. 44
  John, Major .. 24
  Robert 24
  Sam'l 67
Finley
  Sam. 27
Fisher
  Frederick 27
  Jacob 59
Fitch
  Nathaniel 16, 21
Fitzpatrick
  John 12, 31
Fleming
  C. 104

The Mirror, Washington Kentucky   The Eagle, Maysville, Kentucky

Thos. W. 65
Foley
  Henry 41
Follis
  T. 102
  Thomas 102, 104
Ford
  Walter 101, 103
Forentan
  Ezekiel 24
Forwood
  Wm. 59
Foushee
  F. 102, 104
Fowler
  Alexander 49
  J. 101, 103
France
  James 59
Frazer
  Adam 32, 38
Freeman
  C. 39
  Elijah 24
French
  Hugh 87
  John, Capt. ... 44
Fries
  John 8
  Mr. 3
Fritter
  Susanna 59
Fullerton
  James 59
Fulton
  Hugh 24, 59
Fuquee
  Moses 88

G

Gardner

William 24
Garnes
  Benj. B. 59
Garonde
  John 77
Garrard
  Wm. 49
Garrards
  James
    Robinson. 24
Gater
  Cornelius 44
Gayle
  J. 102
  John ... 102, 104
  M. 102
  Matthew 102, 104
Giant
  James 59
Gideon
  Peter 59
Giles
  Ebenezer 45
Gilman
  Benjamin Ives 55
Ginnings
  William 38
Glaves
  William 102, 104
Godbold
  Dr. 91
Goforth
  William,
    Doctor 24
Grainger
  Mr. 24
Grant
  Jesse M. 59
  John 39
  P. 88
  Peter 68

Sq. 42
GRAUL
  Daniel 71
Graves
  John 24
Gray
  Mr. 3
Grayfor
  Robert 44
Grayham
  Mr. 59
  Wm. 59
Grinstead
  Mr. 68
Gunsalus
  Samuel 59
Guthrie
  Alex. 59

H

Hadon
  Mr. 44
Hagaty
  Mrs. 92
Haggin
  Associate
    Justice 82
HALDEMAN
  John 94
Hall
  Benjamin 6
Haller
  John 44
Hamet
  Mr. 99
Hamilton
  George ... 24, 44
Hammat
  Richard 59
Hancock
  Joseph 44

108

The Mirror, Washington Kentucky   The Eagle, Maysville, Kentucky

Handy
  James........... 24
Hanna
  Hugh............ 44
  William......... 24
Hannah
  Hugh............ 79
  William......... 79
Hanson
  John............ 24
Harker
  Richard......... 24
Harp
  Micaijah........ 35
  Wiley........... 35
Harrigan
  Mr.............. 2
Harris
  Ed.............. 12
  James........... 52
  Mr.............. 104
Harrison'
  D. 85
Hart
  Benjamin........ 87
  Thomas.......... 13
Hartung
  Godfried........ 7
  Mrs............. 7
Hasman
  Michael......... 44
Hathaway
  Aaron........... 59
Haughton
  Mr.............. 46
  R. 43
Hawes
  L. L........ 94, 97
  L.L............. 88
Hawke
  Philip.......... 59

Hawkins........... 12
  Col............. 83
  Colonel......... 51
  James B......... 76
  Mr.............. 31
Haworth
  John ... 101, 103
Haynes
  Thomas.......... 44
  Wm.............. 44
Hays
  Notely.......... 44
Hedges
  Samuel.......... 24
  Samuel P........ 44
  Washing. W...... 59
Hedges,
  Mr.............. 26
Hedleston
  William......... 24
Heister
  Mr.............. 26
Helen
  Samuel.......... 59
Henderson
  Jonathan........ 24
Henry
  David........... 44
  Robt. P......... 86
  William......... 36
Heth
  Capt............ 24
Hewitts
  Messrs.......... 94
Hickman
  B. 82
Hill
  Brigadier
    general 47
  John ... 101, 103
  Nathan 44

  Robert.......... 59
Hitchitaw
  Indians......... 50
Hixson
  Thomas .. 61, 80
HOCKADAY
  John............ 73
Hofman
  Michael......... 24
Holdeman
  John............ 76
Holden
  Delana.......... 59
  Edward.......... 59
Holt
  Mr.............. 49
Holton
  Jesse, Rev...... 78
Homes
  Benj............ 59
Hooker
  N. 62
Hopkins
  John............ 36
  Samuel.......... 59
HORNE &
  HITCHISON 61
Hoskins
  Woodruff........ 59
How
  John............ 24
Howard
  Lieut........... 25
Howe
  Perley.......... 55
Hughes
  David........... 30
  James 19, 20
Hughs
  Rowland......... 43
Humphreys

The Mirror, Washington Kentucky   The Eagle, Maysville, Kentucky

Owen 44
Hunt
   Abijah 2
   Jesse 2
   Mashack 24
   Wm. G. 93
Hunter
   Joseph 24
Hunter and
   Beaumont 16
Hutchinson
   Langhorne &
     Hutchinson81
   Langhorne &
     Hutchinsons'
     s 72

I

Indian
   Big Thigh 27
   Black Hoof .. 27
   Bull Head 77
   Pado 64
   Seminoles 77
Indians 3, 19, 22, 30, 35, 63
   Black Feet ... 63
   Chickasaws 30, 33
   Creek 36, 99
   Kaskaskia 2
   Osages 63
   Pawnee 63
   Shawanee 33
   Walk on the
     Water 76
   Wyandott 76
Iredell
   Judge 8
Israel
   Israel 55

J

J & E. G. BYERS 69
Jackson
   Andrew, Gen. 86
   Andrew,
     General ... 63
Jamerson
   Mr. 23
January
   January &
     Sutherland 93
   MARTIN &
     JANUARY 73
   Mr. 69
   Samuel 56, 65, 70
   Samuel Sen'r &
     Co. 79
January, Withans
   & January 68
Jenning
   William 5
John
   Mordica 59
Johnsen
   Aron 24
Johnson
   David 44
   J.T. 86
   James 58
   John 31
   Wm. Anthony 24
Johnston
   Daniel 61, 79
   Martha ... 61, 79
   Mason 39
   Orramel, Dr. .. 56
Jones
   Asberry 59
   Edward 59
   Edward O 59

Ignatius 24
John 10, 18
Joshua 101, 103
Mr. 52
Thomas 65
William 24
Jonny
   Captain 76
Joseph
   Shop keeper in
     Portsmouth 77
Judd
   William 24

K

Keith
   A.D. 83
   John 24
   Thomas 24
Kellay
   James. 55
Kemp
   Captain 9
Kempt
   Captain 9
Kendall
   Philip Richard 66
Kennan
   William .. 10, 18
   William, ... 28
Kennan,
   William 21
Kennedy
   John 24
   William 44
Kenton
   John 44
   Major 27
   Simon 40
Kerr

The Mirror, Washington Kentucky The Eagle, Maysville, Kentucky

Joseph.... 24, 44
Key
  James........... 24
Keys
  William.. 11, 18
Kinds
  Robert.......... 59
Kinnand
  John.............. 50
Knapp
  Samuel......... 59
Knight
  Geo.B. 78

L

Lamb
  Edward 59
Landgford
  Eliza. 59
LANDGHORNE
  & PAYNE 72
Langford
  Mr. 35
Langham
  E. 27
Langhorn
  Maurice 66
Langhorne 71
  Captain 94
  John T. 94
Langhorne &
  Hutchinsons
  XE
  "Hutchinson:
  Langhorne
  &
  Hutchinsons'
  s" 's 72
  M.88
  M. Captain.. 85
Langhorne &

Hutchinson... 81
Langhorne &
  Payne 71
Laughlin
  A. M. 89
Lauraned
  James H. 59
Lawson
  Hannah 88
  James 88
Laycock
  Wm. 76
Leake
  Robert.......... 24
Leath
  James 27
Lee
  Capt. Stephen?81
  D & S. LEE'S
  GROCERY
  STORE ... 72
  General 44
  Henry 20
  Michael........ 57
  Stephen 62
Lewis
  Asa................ 44
  George 5
  John 44
  Mr. 8
  Thomas 50
Light
  Peter............. 24
Lilleston
  R.C. 88
Lindsay
  David 63
Lindsey
  John B. 79
Lisa
  Manuel......... 63

Mr. 63
Logan
  George 13
  John 44
Lowburrow
  Preston S. 82
Lowry
  John 59
Lucas
  Samuel......... 29
Ludlow
  Major 38

M

M'Adow
  John 23
M'Cartty
  James 24
  Samuel......... 43
M'Cartys........... 39
M'Clean
  William 23
M'Clennen
  Wm. 59
M'Clune
  James 24
M'Clure
  Andrew 13
M'Comas
  John 54
M'Conky
  Mr. 47
M'Connel
  Betsey 43
  Hugh 59
M'Connell
  Robert 23
M'Cormick
  William 50
M'Coy
  James 43

111

The Mirror, Washington Kentucky   The Eagle, Maysville, Kentucky

Samuel... 23, 28
M'Donald
 Wm. 59
M'Dougal
 Richard 68
M'Dowell
 Mr. 23
M'Farlin
 John, Major . 34
M'Intire
 John 59
M'Kee
 John 59
M'KEY
 Jesse 81
 Jessee............ 61
M'Kinney
 Cain 42
 John 79
M'Nairy
 Judge 37
M'Namar
 Jenny 24
M'Nevin
 Mr. 34
M'Nutt
 John 76
M'Rea
 Mr. 2
Macgregor
 Alexander 31
Machir
 Henry 68
 John 5, 45
 Mr. 31
Mackey
 William 72
Mackoy
 John 88
Maddox
 Zorababel 24

Zorabable..... 44
Mahan
 John 16, 21
Makateywekashaw27
Malatt
 Catherine 79
 Daniel 79
M'Alexander
 James . 101, 103
 John ... 101, 103
Malone
 John 24
 Mr. 92
Malott
 John 59
Marshal
 Thomas, Junr. 40
Marshall
 A. K. 93
 Alexander K. 44
 J. J................ 93
 Thomas 6, 12, 13, 44
 Thomas, Jun.18, 19, 24
Martin
 Edmund 44
 Jeremiah 59
 MARTIN &
  JANUARY73
Mason
 James 5, 6
 John 5, 6
 S.T. 36
Massey
 Henry 24
 Nathaniel 24
Massie
 Col. 4, 11
 D. 73
 David 66
Matthews
 George 87

Maxsie
 David 76
Mayhall
 Timothy........ 24
Mayo
 Mr. 43
Maysville Meeting 85
Mayuugh
 Michael 59
McCleary
 Wm. 11
McCluney
 W. 55
M'Cleary
 Wm. 17
M'Connel
 F. 102
M'Connell
 F. 104
Meck
 Mary 5
 Robert 5
Meeker &
 Cochran6, 13, 18
Meredith
 Samuel 20
Metcalf
 Mr. 24
Metcalfe
 Charles......... 20
 Eli 20
 Mr. 92
Miles
 John 42
Miller
 Jacin............. 59
 Jane 79
 Mirror 19
Mitchel
 George 44
Mitchell

The Mirror, Washington Kentucky   The Eagle, Maysville, Kentucky

A. 74
George......... 49
Laban........... 60
Lavan........... 60
Mollyneaux
   Miss............. 89
   Mr............... 89
Monroe
   Thomas B. ... 82
Montgomery
   James........... 55
Moor
   H. 84
   Robert.......... 79
Moore
   Ann............... 59
   Benjamin..... 59
   George101, 103
   Harbin, Hon. 83
   Joseph59, 101, 103
   Lewis............ 34
   Lewis, Major24, 44
   Mary............ 24
   Richard101, 103
   Stanfield 76
   T.P................ 86
Moreland
   Wm.............. 97
Morford
   John............. 87
Morgan
   Charles20, 101, 103
Morris
   Daniel, Capt. 36
   James........... 66
   Mr................ 53
Morrison
   David..... 71, 89
   J. 71
   James24, 44, 69, 72
   Mr. D............. 94

Morrison &
   Mackey........ 72
Morrison &
   Vertner......... 25
Morton
   Robert B. 11, 18
   Mosby............... 12
   J. 102
   L. 102, 104
   Wade.. 102, 104
Mountjoy
   Thomas........ 59
Muhlenberg
   Mr................. 53
Mullanphy
   John........ 24, 44
Murphy
   John............. 59
Murray
   Michael........ 52
   Mr................. 64
Murry
   Michael........ 52

N

Nasawashigaw.. 27
Nat. Poyntz & Co89
Nathan Smith &
   Co................ 59
NEGRO
   Ben.............. 61
   Billy............. 16
   Blage 46
   Bob.............. 41
   Charles......... 41
   Louis............ 31
   Major........... 24
   Man 87
   Man and
      Woman.... 97
   Mary 32

Phill 24
Thomas Smith44
Woman.........87
Woman & 3
   children ...90
Negroe
   Allice...........43
   Woman........42
Negros ..10, 39, 53
Neinimsic..........35
Nelson
   Doctor..........90
   Rev. Mr. 7
   William101, 103
New
   Mr. 3
Newton
   Orrice...........59
Nicholas
   John 32
Nickols
   Mr. 24
Nudegate
   William 28

O

O'Connor
   Arthur 34
O'Hara
   James 2
Odaniel
   John ...101, 103
Old
   Mr. 69
Olney
   Ethan............76
Orr
   Alexander D.,
      Col. 36
   Mr. 54
Orr's Mill..........25

The Mirror, Washington Kentucky

Orry
　Archabald 59
Overfield
　Abner 24
Owens
　Athelstan 69
　William 6

P

Palmer
　Philip 87
Parent
　Samuel 45
Parker
　Alexander, Col.24
　Margaret 59
　Thomas 97
　William 31
　Winsloe 49
Parker?
　Thomas 74
Patch
　Joseph 45
Patrick
　John ... 102, 104
Patten
　James 3
Patterson
　David. 101, 103
　James 44
　Nathaniel 24
Patton
　John 44
Paxton
　Jas. A. 66
Payne 71
　Benj. 59
　Edward 24
　Jno. N. 99
　LANDGHORN
　　E & PAYNE72

The Eagle, Maysville, Kentucky

Thomas Y. 94
Pearle
　William 38
　William, Jun. 38
Peers
　Valentine 44
　Vall, Major ... 44
Pelham
　C. 18
　Charles 11, 17, 21, 29, 80
Pemberton
　Bennett 6
Pendleton
　Philip 11, 17
Perkins
　Thomas 101, 103
Perry
　James . 101, 103
　John ... 101, 103
Peters
　David 59
　Judge 32
　Sarah 59
Philips
　George 44
Phillips
　Wm. B. 68
Phillips & Stout 60
Physick
　Dr. 92
Pickett
　John 24
Pigot 51
Pleasants
　John 42
Poage
　George 73
　Robert 44
Pogue
　Robert 19
Porter

Cam 98
N.S. 78
Potter
　Thomas 50
Powel
　Samuel 41
Powers
　James 59, 61, 81
　Robert 44
POYNTZ
　William M. ... 73
Pralston
　Ezekiel 44
Preston
　John 52
Primen
　James . 101, 103
Putnam
　Edwin 55
Pyane
　John 82
Pysiz
　William M. ... 65

Q

Quantance.
　Wiliam (sic) . 21

R

Rachford
　Robert 44
Rains
　John 79
Ralston
　Ezekiel 44
　Jonathan 44
Ramsay
　B. 4
　Col. 90
　Mr. 13
Randolph

The Mirror, Washington Kentucky   The Eagle, Maysville, Kentucky

Mr. 3	Robb	Christian 8
Rankin	Jos. 62	John 50
Col. 22	Samuel 59	**S**
Mr. 54	Robbins	
Ransom	Jonathan 45, 48, 53	Samuel
A. 78	Mr. 51	Giles 6
Rawlings	Roberts	Sanders
Cardiff T. 59	Benjamin 32	James 24
Nathan 34	Robertson	Lewis 82
Rea	Dr. 90	Sanderson
Geo. 90	John 87	Cyrus 88
Reddington	Wm. B. 59	John 66
Samuel 76	Robetson	Sargent
Redmond	Dr. 91	James 24
Elijah 59	Robinson	Savage
Reed	John, Junr. 31	John 59
William 24	John, Senr. ... 39	Savary
Reeves	William 24	J. 41
Nathan, Captain	Roe	Schiffer
.... 26	John, P.M. 60	Henry 8
Reid	Rogers	Schneider
Walker 61	Jane 24	Mr. 25
Rice	Rollf	Schwartz
George 102, 104	Ellinner 27	Daniel 8
Martha 24	Hazzen 27	Scot
Mr. 104	Roper	John 44
Phinebas G. .. 59	William P. 65	Scott
Richards	Ross	James 34
Wm. 59	Richard 39	Seagrove
Ricketts	Rowland	James 51
R., Jr. 89	Thomas 59	Mr. 51
Ridenhour	Rudd	Selley
Mr. 64	Thomas, Capt. 98	Leah 24
Ridgley	Rumford	SEYBOLD
Noah 57	Jonathan. 40, 54	Demsey 65
Riley	Rumsey	Shackleford
James 59	Charles 59	Doctor 94
Ritchey	Rush	James 90, 99
Adam 44	Dr. 92	W.B. 66
Ritter	Judge 26	William B. 71, 80
Richard 56	Ruth	Shamber

115

The Mirror, Washington Kentucky The Eagle, Maysville, Kentucky

Captain 7
Shannon meeting
  house 85
Sharp
  David 44
  S.P. 82
  Solomon P. .. 82
Shaw
  Nathaniel 24
Shawnanee 27
Shawnees 35
Sheffers
  George 8
Shelton
  James 59
Shepard
  Samuel B. 59
Shepherd
  Adam 37
Shoenberger
  P. 88
  Peter 88, 99
Shotwell
  Jno. 66
  Mr. 24
SHUTZ, HIXSON
  & Co. 62
Shy
  James 87
Siminolias
  Indians 51
Simpson
  Jno. Simpson &
    Co. 92
Sinclair
  Mr. 29
Skillern
  William 101, 103
  slave
    George 93
Sloo

Mr. 54
Thomas 5
Smith
  Alex. 5
  Anne 5
  Kisziah 43
  Nathan 59
  Robert 41
  Rulef 59
  Thomas 44
  William 43
Sneed
  Achilles 82
  Mr. 82, 83
Soward
  Richard 24
SPENCER
  Mrs. 57
Spurrier
  Joseph 59
St. Clair
  Wm. 59
Stahler
  Henry 8
Starr
  Swan & Starr 94
Steel
  Wm. 59
Steele
  Jacob 50
Steers
  Thomas 59
Stephens
  James 75
Stephenson
  Joseph 24
  Rebekah 24
Sterrit
  John 50
Stewart
  John 25

John, Jun. 25
Levin 59, 74
Peter A.G. 79
Stickland
  Allen 45
Stockton
  Joshua 23, 28, 65
  Maj. George ... 4
Stocton
  George 32
Stone
  James 76
Stout
  Jonathan 32
  Platt 92
Stratton
  Aaron 24
  Arron 73
Sullivant
  Lucas 44
SUMMERS
  Thomas 61
Sumrall
  J.K. 71
  Jno. 81
  John 66
  Jos. K. 81
Sutherland
  January &
    Sutherland 93
  Wm. 88
Sutton
  John 25
  William 25
Swan
  Swan & Starr 94
Swann
  Mr. 47
Sweezy
  Mr. 29, 30
Swigert

The Mirror, Washington Kentucky The Eagle, Maysville, Kentucky

T

Tabb
- John 10, 17
Talbot
- Davis B. 76
TALBOTT
- Daniel 70
Talirerro
- Nicholas 44
Tandy
- Gabriel 78
TAPP
- Elias 70
Tatham
- C. 49
Taylor
- Col. R. 82
- Francis 5, 24, 28, 44
- Frank 24
- Hubard 6
- James 79
- John 19, 24, 34, 44
- Mr. 24
- Robert 68, 97
- William 42
Tebbs
- D. 54
- Mrs. 9
- S. 54
- Samuel 9
Terel 12
Terrel
- Mr. 31
Tharpe
- Thomas 102
Thomas
- ? 4
- Henry 79
- Jacob 31

- Jacob 82
- John 79
- Philemon 10, 17, 44
- Rees 79
- Silas 79
- Wm. P. 59
Thompson
- George B. 22
- George H. 22
- John ... 4, 11, 44
- William 44
Thomson
- George 16
Thornton
- Anthony 6
- Presly, Captain 6
- Resly 6
Tilton
- Enoch M. 87
- Richard 16, 21, 24, 50
TIMBERLAKE
- Henry. 102, 104
- Ob'd S. 73
Tinker
- W. 88
Tolle
- James 59
Tom
- Mr. 44
Toulmin.
- Harry 28
Treacle
- Stephen 24
Tribbey
- John 59
Trigg
- J. 3
Trimble
- Associate
  - Justice 82
Triplett

- Thomas 82
Tully
- John 35
TUREMAN
- Henry C. 88
- William & son 72

U

Urmston
- Benjamin 26

V

Van Amburgh
- Benjamin 54
- Betsy 54
Vandeventer
- Peter 59
Vanhorne
- Mr. 64
Verner
- Alexander 24
Vertner
- Daniel 24
Vicker
- Dr. 91
Viers
- Frederick C. .. 59
Vincent
- Thomas 59
Violett
- Mr. 93

W

Waggoner
- O. G. 82
Walden
- John 20
Walker
- Fran. 78
- M. 102, 104

The Mirror, Washington Kentucky   The Eagle, Maysville, Kentucky

Mr. 53
W. 102
William 102, 104
Wm. 60
Wallace
   Thomas 65
   William 44
Waller
   John 44
Wallingsford
   Joseph 60
Walls
   Elisha 60
Walters
   Josephus 42, 44
Walton
   John 24
   Simeon 60
Ward
   Col. 27
   William 20
   William, Col. 33
Waring
   R.W. 46
   Thomas 5, 27
Washington
   William 24
Watkins
   John ... 102, 104
   Joseph 101, 103
   Nicholas 102, 104
   Robert 102, 104
   Thomas 101, 103
   Wm. 60
Weaver
   T. 102, 104
   Tilman 102, 104
Webb
   Black & Webb 92
Wells
   Abraham

William ... 24
West
   Francis 101, 103
   William, Capt. 24
Whitaker
   James 41
White
   George 60
   H. 89
Whitington
   Joshua 60
Whittercher
   John 44
Wiatt
   William 47
Wickliffe
   C.A. 86
Wickliffee
   C.A. 86
Wier
   Henry 60
Wiggins
   Archibald 11, 17
Wilcox
   Messrs 53
Wilkey
   Francis A 60
Wilkins
   John 2
Wilkinson
   Melinda **87**
Williams
   Abram 44
   George 60
   Henry 60
   Isaac 48
   Nathan 44
   Oliver 76
   Richard 44
   Thomas 32
   Thoms O., Dr. 96

Willis
   William T. 85
   Wm. T. 86
Willmann
   Christian 39
Wills
   I.S. 49
Wilson
   James 44, 45
   John 60
   Mr. 47
   Robert 24
   Robert, Rev. . 65
   Sally 60
Wilson & Swann 42
Winchel
   Oliver 60
Winn
   John 4, 12
   Mr. 13
Witham
   Mr. 69
Withans
   January,
     Withans &
     January 68
Woddy
   Will. ... 101, 103
Woffor
   Benjamin 39
Wood
   Archibald 101, 103
   George 31
   James 5
   John 5, 52
   Joseph 45
   Katy 5
   Mary 5
   William 27
   William, Revd. 24
   Wm. 11, 18

Wood's
  Mountpleasant
  Mills............ 18
Woodhouse
  Wm.............. 60
Woodson
  H. 78
Woodward
  William........ 39
Woodworth
  Jared........... 60
Worthington
  Thomas........ 24
Wossor
  Benjamin..... 39
Wright
  Elizabeth...... 79
  William........ 79

Y

Yancy
  Charles 102, 104

Mr. 104
Yeartes
  Judge............ 14
Yeatman
  Thomas........ 93
Yoder
  Henry.......... 60
Young
  A. 78
  Robert.......... 66

www.ingramcontent.com/pod-product-compliance
Lightning Source LLC
Chambersburg PA
CBHW050649160426
43194CB00010B/1867